Advance pra...
The Customer Servic...

"Rich Gallagher explores the daunting tas[...] [...]g with your most difficult customers in *The Customer Service Survival Kit*. This invaluable book provides service professionals of all levels with a clear framework of how to anticipate customer expectations and turn customer service nightmares into winning situations—every time!"

> **—Carolyn Healey, Publisher, SupportIndustry.com and RecognizeServiceExcellence.com**

"When the worst-case scenarios happen, as they often do when serving customers, this book is a lifesaver! Knowing what to say, when to say it and how to say it will be the difference between having a former customer and a loyal customer!"

> **—Randi Busse, President and Founder of Workforce Development Group, Inc.**

"What is the key to great customer service? Rich Gallagher shows how to confidently handle even the worst customer service issues!"

> **—Barry Moltz, author of *Bounce!* and *Small Town Rules***

"Just when I thought I had seen it all and learned as much as I could from Rich, he proves me wrong. The examples alone will give you reason to pick up the book time and time again."

> **—Phil Verghis, Chief Everything Officer, The Verghis Group, and author of *The Ultimate Customer Support Executive***

"If you've delivered any sort of service to customers, you know bad things sometimes happen to good customers. But there's never been a guide to handle these problems—until now. Rich Gallagher penned THE ultimate guide to what happens when things go wrong—and they will go wrong! This book is filled with useful insights even the most experienced customer service professional can learn from. Run—don't walk—to get your copy today."

> **—Phil Gerbyshak, Chief Connections Officer and author of four books and over 2,000 articles on customer service, social media, and more**

"Rich Gallagher is a customer service rock star!"

> **—Prof. Susan Stafford, Chair of Hotel and Restaurant Management, SUNY TC3**

THE
Customer Service
Survival Kit

THE
Customer Service
Survival Kit

What to Say to Defuse Even the Worst Customer Situations

Richard S. Gallagher

Foreword by Carol Roth

AMACOM
AMERICAN MANAGEMENT ASSOCIATION
New York • Atlanta • Brussels • Chicago • Mexico City • San Francisco
Shanghai • Tokyo • Toronto • Washington, D.C.

Bulk discounts available. For details visit:
www.amacombooks.org/go/specialsales
Or contact special sales:
Phone: 800-250-5308
Email: specialsls@amanet.org
View all the AMACOM titles at: www.amacombooks.org

Library of Congress Cataloging-in-Publication Data

Gallagher, Richard S.
    The customer service survival kit : what to say to defuse even the worst customer situations / Richard S. Gallagher.
      pages   cm
    Includes bibliographical references and index.
      ISBN 978-0-8144-3183-2 (pbk.)—ISBN 0-8144-3183-6 (pbk.)   1. Customer services.   2. Customer relations.   I. Title.
    HF5415.5.G3468   2013
    658.8'12—dc23

                                                                    2012040797

About AMA

American Management Association (www.amanet.org) is a world leader in talent development, advancing the skills of individuals to drive business success. Our mission is to support the goals of individuals and organizations through a complete range of products and services, including classroom and virtual seminars, webcasts, webinars, podcasts, conferences, corporate and government solutions, business books, and research. AMA's approach to improving performance combines experiential learning—learning through doing—with opportunities for ongoing professional growth at every step of one's career journey.

Printing number

10 9 8 7 6 5 4 3 2 1

To Colleen, my joy and my soul mate

Contents

Contents

Chapter 10   The Wrap-Up   105

PART III   YOUR WORST CUSTOMER SITUATIONS—SOLVED!   113

· · · · · · · · · ·

Chapter 11   You're the Boss   115

Chapter 12   Don't You Know Who I Am?   121

Chapter 13   The Concert That Never Was   125

Chapter 14   I'll Be Suing You   131

Chapter 15   Quelling a Social Media Firestorm   135

Chapter 16   Just Plane Terrible   139

Foreword

· ·

COMMUNICATION IS AN ART as well as a science. In our modern world of texts, tweets, and emails, coupled with a general oversaturation of information, I believe that communication has actually become a lost art. However, that lost art is about to be reclaimed.

In *The Customer Service Survival Kit: What to Say to Defuse Even the Worst Customer Situations*, Rich Gallagher masterfully helps you conquer this lost art form, which will not only help you turn around virtually any customer issue but also give you the nuanced skills to be able to communicate effectively with just about anyone.

While communication as an art form may be lost, it has become more important than ever. Today's crowded business landscape is extremely competitive, and although it may be easier to superficially reach customers, they are bombarded with so much information that it is difficult to break through the noise. In addition, it is easy for customers to affect your business with their opinions. Myriad outlets, from blogs to review sites to social media, allow customers to share their thoughts about your business, regardless of whether that feedback is accurate or warranted. So your ability to solve issues quickly and effectively—and to plain avoid them in the first place—is one of the greatest assets you and your team can leverage for success.

I'm a tough customer when it comes to books (well truthfully, to just about anything), and I loved this book. Rich Gallagher is one of the best communicators around, and he has a deep, credible background as a writer, communications skills expert, and psychotherapist. *The Customer Service Survival Kit* is everything you would want in a business book: It's well written, easy to understand, and, most importantly, relevant and helpful. Plus, I think it's more than a business book, as the communication lessons within can apply to almost any personal or professional situation.

I'm always amazed at how much of what we say gets lost in translation, especially in a world where everyone seems to be tuned in to their favorite radio station, WIIFM (What's in It for Me). However, what's so powerful about communication and the lessons in this book is that the same information can resonate differently with a slight tweak in approach and perspective, clever rephrasing, or just extending some desired empathy.

If you are anything like me, you may have a burning desire to want to explain and show to people what is "right." But to be successful in any relationship—personal or business-oriented—it is critical to remember the goals. Unfortunately, being right as a goal rarely gets you the best outcome. *The Customer Service Survival Kit* gives you a framework to set beneficial goals up front, as well as the tools to meet those goals successfully.

I don't make recommendations often, because I take them very seriously, but I can confidently say that you'll get a significant return on investment from reading and implementing the advice and strategies in this book, and will likely refer back to it for years to come. Wishing you continued success,

CAROL ROTH
Recovering investment banker, business strategist,
and *New York Times* bestselling author of *The Entrepreneur Equation*
www.CarolRoth.com
Twitter: @CarolJSRoth

Acknowledgments

· ·

THIS BOOK WAS TRULY CO-CREATED with the help of a lot of great people. Here are just a few of them:

Fellow business author Carol Roth, for whom I am a contributing blogger on CarolRoth.com, went far above and beyond the call of duty to help make this book happen. She was more than generous in offering her support, the resources of her blog community, and even her cousin (airline manager Jeff Greenman, mentioned in Chapter 1), as well as writing this book's foreword. I owe her great blogs for at least the next decade.

Carolyn Healey, publisher of leading customer support portal site SupportIndustry.com as well as customer service site RecognizeService Excellence.com, has been my partner in crime for many years. Much of the idea for this book came from her survey research on critical customer scenarios and effective training approaches, and our joint webinars have been a valuable testing ground for sharing my ideas with thousands of customer support professionals.

Of all the people I have the pleasure of presenting for, I have to single out Todd Lewis, Veronica Puailoa, and the entire team at Citrix GoToAssist for regularly providing me with a great public platform in front of service-industry leaders worldwide. They are visionaries, and I feel honored to partner with them.

Bob Nirkind, my editor at AMACOM Books, has been a phenomenal cheerleader for this project since its inception and a delight to work with. It was his idea to crowdsource many of the examples in this book using social media. It has been an honor and a pleasure to work with the entire team at AMACOM on our fourth book project together. And a special thanks to my longtime literary agent, Diana Finch, who first planted the seed for this project, for a great working relationship.

Numerous people contributed their expertise and/or examples of challenging customer situations, including Lieutenant Chauncey Bennett III of the New York State University Police, retired Cornell University police officer Janice Pack, communications-skills author John Kador, colleague and speaker extraordinaire Julie Kowalski, psychologist Dr. Nancy Davis, FBI chaplain Dennis Hayes, Gina Schreck of SynapseConnecting, Professor Jeremy Cooperstock of McGill University, Sara Schoonover of TicketKick, Janet Christy of Leverage and Development LLC, Karlene Sinclair-Robinson of KSR Solutions LLC, Jim Josselyn of the Academy of Music and Drama, Stacy Robin of The Degania Group, and Ryan Crichett of RMC TECH Mobile Repair. Thank you all for being part of this project.

My wife, Colleen, has always been my editor, my sounding board, and the person I am madly in love with. You are the light of my life. Thank you for being you.

Finally, I would like to tip my hat to the organizations I have worked for in my own career in customer service and support, and the thousands of people I speak to every year. The things I have learned from you over the years have been a precious gift, and this book is a small attempt to return the favor. Enjoy!

THE
Customer Service Survival Kit

Introduction

I LOVE worst-case scenarios.

Why? Because they hold the key to creating truly incredible service.

Think about it. There is a lot of bad service out there. And most of it happens because people who serve the public constantly fear the worst, and then react to everyone from a defensive posture. Scratch the surface of most disengaged people who serve the public, and more often than not you will find fear lurking there. They feel alone and vulnerable on a very public stage, worrying about when the next customer will leave them twisting defenselessly in the wind.

When service providers don't bother to ask you what you want, it is often because they are afraid they won't be able to handle what you tell them. When they tell you "no," they are hiding behind their policies because they have no idea how to negotiate with you. Even though they wear name tags that say "Hi, Can I Help You?" they are silently praying you will just go away creating as little damage as possible. And when you demand to speak to a manager, they often pass you off to someone who is as frightened and as clueless as they are.

So how do you change this fear? By teaching people the skills that hostage negotiators, crisis counselors, psychotherapists, and police officers use in their worst situations. When people learn these skills, everything changes. They become supremely confident in any situation. They can really engage customers, because they know they are able to lean back on these communications skills for anything someone might throw at them. It is here, in this zone of incredible confidence, that greatness takes root.

I know this works because I have watched it happen over and over.

Let me share a little about myself. I am a former customer support executive who is now a public speaker as well as a practicing marriage and family therapist. My specialty is teaching people what to say in their most difficult situations. (In other words, when I am not busy having people get angry at me onstage in front of large audiences, I put myself in the middle of other people's family conflicts—go figure!)

Before I did that, I had a reputation for dramatically turning around the performance of customer-contact operations: creating near-perfect customer-satisfaction ratings, near-zero turnover, and record sales. It was here that I discovered the incredible power of the worst-case scenario. I found that when you teach people how to handle these worst cases, they become superstars. And when you teach *everyone* on a team how to handle them, the results are truly magical.

Worst-case situations are defined by a customer's extreme reaction, no matter what actually happened. This book will teach you how to handle these situations calmly and professionally. Many of the book's examples will walk you through scenarios where the stakes are high, where people are completely unreasonable, or where someone is hopping mad and you are totally, utterly at fault. Others will examine routine situations where the wrong words could ignite a confrontation, and the right words can prevent one. You will learn how to walk safely into all of these discussions, defuse them with the skill of a bomb squad, and send everyone away feeling better.

Best of all, you don't need to become braver, smarter, or craftier. You just need to use different words that I will teach you, step-by-step, using scenarios many of us lie awake at night worrying about. These words come from very recent, empirical principles of communications psychology that trigger the way other people think and feel.

Using real-life dialogues and chapter exercises, including an appendix with my solutions, you will learn the same communications skills that I teach in my live training programs.

There is just one catch to learning these skills: You must be prepared to take your human nature and stand it on its head. Instead of defending yourself, you will learn how to lean into criticism with gusto. Rather than minimizing the consequences of something, you will learn how to out-dramatize an angry customer and to take catchphrases like "I understand" and banish them forever. You will also learn to challenge your assumptions about difficult customers. It will be a wild ride in spots.

Here is why the ride will be worth it. Techniques like these spring from the relatively new field of strength-based communications, which has swept areas like athletic coaching, psychotherapy, and business leadership like a tidal wave in recent years—because it works. And when you see how well it works in your most difficult customer situations, it will become clear why all those years of telling yourself and your team to be "nicer" never changed anything. When you get rid of the fear that sits behind most human interactions, you will find an authentic core of confidence that drives great service.

When we first ask people how they would handle really tough situations in our training courses, they often reply, "We'd ask our boss to handle it." In this book, you are the boss. And by learning and practicing these skills, you stand a good chance of becoming the boss in real life, if you aren't one already. Leaders often stand out because of their ability to resolve conflict, and you are about to join the club.

There is one more reason for learning how to handle your worst customer situations. These skills will affect the rest of your life in a big way. They will change the way you communicate with your supervisors, your coworkers, your children, and your life partner. (Trust me on this one—I have been together with mine for nearly forty years.) When you know how to make it safe to talk about anything, you get an added bonus of trust, intimacy, and goodwill that fundamentally changes your relationships with others.

Your cost for all of these benefits? You just need to be prepared to look at your worst customer situations differently, with an open mind, and be willing to put these techniques to work. They take practice, but in time they will become a natural part of who you are. And then you will discover, as I have, how your worst customers can become the best friends your service career ever had.

PART I

Why Worst-Case Scenarios Matter

CHAPTER 1

Understanding the "Uh-Oh" Moment

I AM STANDING IN FRONT of hundreds of people, microphone in hand, on the stage of an auditorium. I ask the audience a simple question, one of many I will ask that morning. But this is the only one that instantly causes nearly every single one of hundreds of hands to shoot into the air:

"Have you ever had a customer situation that went really, really wrong?"

When you scratch the surface of any group of people who work with the public, you will hear a truly amazing litany of war stories. Physical and verbal intimidation. Outrageous demands. Letters telling your boss how horrible you are. Threats of lawsuits. Or perhaps the thing many of us fear the most: devastating consequences for a customer that were your fault.

These are what I call the "uh-oh" moments: unplanned, unscripted, and often extreme situations. Moments where good intentions are not enough, and human nature fails us. It is in these moments that the sunshine-and-smile training school of customer service collides with the real world. They do not happen very often. Hopefully they are just a small fraction of the situations you deal with across your career. But if you work with customers long enough, like nearly half of all people working today, they will eventually happen to you.

That is where this book comes in. It will not teach you how to be "nice." It will not help you have a good attitude. And it will not discuss basic customer relationship skills that your mother probably taught you when you were six. Instead, in this book we are going to arm you with tools to handle your very worst customer situations—tools that people like crisis counselors, hostage negotiators, psychotherapists, and others use to gain control of these situations. In the process, you will discover how to become supremely confident in *any* customer situation, and fundamentally change the way you deal with the public.

Why Worst-Case Scenarios Are Important

Worst-case scenarios can be frightening and challenging. Yet at the same time, they happen pretty infrequently for most people; I would say no more than a fraction of a percent of our overall transactions, based on my informal surveys of speaking audiences. So if this is the case, why should we bother learning to handle them? Can't we just call in our boss, or suffer through them when they happen?

I have a different view. I personally believe that learning how to handle your worst customer situations is the single most important skill you can learn in your career, and that teaching your team these skills is the surest way to succeed as a leader. Here are three reasons why:

1. These are all teachable skills, and most people do not know them until they are taught them. For example, years ago I had no idea what I might say to someone threatening suicide. Now I *do* know because of the skills I was taught when I worked on a crisis line. Once you have learned how to manage crisis and conflict, these skills stick with you for the rest of your life.

2. Learning to handle your worst situations is the key to delivering excellent service *all* of the time. It is the secret weapon that most smile-training books never talk about. Wherever I worked, it was our single biggest tool in changing the way we dealt with customers.

3. These skills change *you*. Shakespeare wrote, "Cowards die many times before their deaths, / The valiant never taste of

death but once." When you feel supremely confident walking into any customer situation, your view of your job—and life itself—changes dramatically.

Do you ever wonder why so many employees act rude, snippy, and disengaged? Why companies that seemingly want your business employ people who act like they are off in another zip code somewhere? Why entire companies sometimes fail to do the right thing?

It isn't because these people's shorts are all too tight. More often than you think, it is because they constantly operate from a defensive posture, driven by a fear of what might go wrong. They constantly have their shields up and their swords drawn, even in the most innocent encounters, which is why pushing them to be nicer never works: You haven't taken that core fear away.

This is why customer-contact teams I managed did so incredibly well after they learned how to manage crisis situations. I didn't ask them to smile more often, change their personalities, or work harder. Instead, I simply taught them how to execute in the worst situations they could imagine. Then these people, who had just about every personality on the face of the earth, had the skills and confidence to make each customer feel fantastic, no matter what the situation. And yes, they also shone in a crisis.

Nowadays I speak to thousands of people a year all over North America, helping them understand and manage their worst customer situations. Wherever I go, I see the same thing. Nearly everyone, from entry-level employees to senior executives, handles serious conflict the same way—like deer frozen in the headlights—until they are taught what to say and do. Then magic starts to happen. So now, let's look at a sample of this magic in action.

What Would You Do?

My good friend and colleague, speaker, and trainer extraordinaire Julie Kowalski had an experience that ranks up there as one of the worst service experiences I have heard of. I don't think I could make up a situation as poorly handled as what actually happened to her.

Julie was planning a family vacation to Hawaii, and being a busy public speaker, she decided to order her vacation clothes from a regional store near where she lived. The store promised the clothes would arrive well before her vacation. They didn't. And as she called, day after day, the store kept promising they would arrive "tomorrow."

Finally, the last "tomorrow" came. Julie was waiting for the cab to the airport with her empty suitcases, and the clothes still didn't arrive. She reluctantly took off for Hawaii, planning to buy a few things when she got there. Meanwhile, the store finally delivered the clothes later that day, dropping off exactly two of everything she had ordered and charging her twice as much as she had expected. When she arrived in Hawaii, she discovered that her credit card was maxed out. She spent a week in paradise with no clothes and no credit.

After she got home, she called the store and was told by a snippy employee that she would have to document what happened in writing. So she did, in the form of a fourteen-page letter that she had her assistant fax to the store—over, and over, and over, and over again.

Now, how would you like to have been the lucky employee who had to respond to my friend Julie?

A manager from this retailer did, in fact, call her back, and according to Julie, she nailed it perfectly. (So well, in fact, that Julie's assistant later wondered why she didn't hear any yelling or arguing after putting the call through.) These were the first words out of this manager's mouth:

"I read your letter, Julie. After everything we have put you through, I can't believe that you are still giving us an opportunity to make things right. I want to learn more about what happened, and see what we can do to repair the damage we have done here."

There is a great deal of psychology going on in an opening like this. Here are some of the things that this manager accomplished with this opening statement:

➤ She let Julie know that she had read her complaint, and then demonstrated it by sharing her disgust at the situation.

➤ She used Julie's name.

➤ She preemptively matched Julie's level of emotion.

➤ She framed Julie's response—which, remember, had consisted of angrily faxing a long letter over and over—as that of a reasonable person.

➤ She took a posture of serving Julie rather than defending herself.

Then, as Julie recounted her grievances, this manager clearly acknowledged and restated each of them in turn. Whether she had unusually good intuition or had been well trained (I suspect both), she succeeded in turning a potentially explosive encounter into a rational discussion.

To its credit, the store did a good job of service recovery. It refunded all of my friend's money, told her to keep the clothes for free as a gesture of apology, and promised to investigate what happened. But before any of this could happen, the road to recovery was paved by saying the right thing when the situation demanded it.

Good Intentions Are Not Enough

You may be thinking to yourself, "I am a pretty smart person. I am also a very nice person. I am good with people. And I can think on my feet. Those skills should get me through most difficult customer situations, right?"

Wrong.

As much as I deeply respect nice people, being nice is not the same as knowing the right words to say in a crisis. In fact, my experience with employees is that these skills have much less to do with whether you are a "people person" and much more to do with how well you have been trained and coached.

Here is a pop quiz to show you what I mean. Let's say that a customer is furious because she was not allowed in to see a major concert the night before because of a misunderstanding over whether her ticket was valid. Take a moment to write down what you would *first* say to her.

_____

_____

_____

Now, answer the following questions:

- ➤ Did you use the phrase "I understand" in your response? As you will learn, this is a dated catchphrase that is as likely to enrage your customer as soothe her.

- ➤ Did you try, even a tiny bit, to explain what might have happened? For many people, this is the first club out of their bag. But you will learn that explaining things too soon serves no purpose and only makes the other person more upset.

- ➤ Did you start by offering to do something to make up for this? That may seem like a good response, but if it was the first thing out of your mouth—without first making sure she feels acknowledged and asking good questions—you may actually be setting her up to escalate her demands further.

Chapter 13 presents a case study that explains how to handle this situation. For now, here is a quick summary: Mirror the gravity of her complaint, ask questions to learn what happened, and validate her statements every time she speaks. Then explore what she feels needs to be done to make this situation right and negotiate an appropriate level of service recovery.

Some of you reading this may have responded the same way. Good for you! But many of you, no matter how nice you are, will have said things that were ineffective or even harmful. And some of you might have struggled with what to say at all.

This is the heart of the "uh-oh" moment: When we most need to be present in a customer's situation, the majority of us say the wrong things or turn into a block of ice. That's because we are uncomfortable and often frightened. And more to the point, because we really don't know what to say. A lot of bad service, especially in a crisis, happens because we simply haven't been taught the right words to say in critical situations. Even some of the world's biggest companies say the wrong things in a crisis, with examples as close as your nightly news.

One of the best analogies I can think of to this situation is acting. Most of us think we can do it. It looks natural when we see it. But when you observe professional actors carrying out a scene more closely, they aren't up there being themselves: They are executing a series of well-rehearsed individual steps. They are positioning themselves at specific chalk lines on the stage, waiting for precise moments to deliver a line, and timing their moves. If you or I took the stage and tried to repeat their scenes, we would appear clumsy and amateurish—just like most of us do in critical customer service situations.

Perhaps an even better comparison is police work. When officers receive a call about a burglary in progress, the police I know don't clasp their heads in their hands and moan, "Oh, my goodness, someone is stealing something!" Instead, they hop into their patrol car and do what they have been trained over and over to do. These officers are masterful at defusing a crisis because they have been taught to do so. And with the right training, you can learn to defuse your crises with customers as well.

What to Say When the Unthinkable Happens

When Jeff Greenman kissed his wife and drove to work one sunny September morning as a manager for a major U.S. airline, he had no idea that by the end of that day, two of his company's planes would crash at the hands of terrorists, all air traffic in the United States would be shut down, and he would be rushed to a crash site to work with victims' families for weeks. How did he personally handle the aftermath of the September 11, 2001, tragedy? As a trained member of his airline's Special Assistance Team, he walked into this situation having a very clear sense of how he would interact with people, using tools such as these:

> ➤ Asking open-ended questions to assess what people needed

> ➤ Acknowledging and paraphrasing what people said

> ➤ Using focusing questions to shift into problem solving

> ➤ Never saying "no," but instead responding in terms of what he *could* do

> ➤ Letting people know that whatever they were thinking and feeling was OK

Jeff had a process to what he was doing, not just good intentions. He knew how to respond to anger, tears, and outrageous demands. He knew how to help people feel heard and supported in some of the worst moments of their lives. Over the weeks he spent with the families of 9/11, he built relationships that benefitted them and his airline's reputation. In fact, he describes his biggest challenge as a positive one: disengaging from all the good relationships he built with these families as he returned to his regular duties.

This is the heart and soul of how to handle a crisis with a customer: Be trained, be prepared, and then know how to execute when a crisis happens. When you become good at it, you still care very much about your customers, but the mechanics of what to do become, in a sense, another day at the office.

The rest of this book explores specific skills you can use in a customer crisis, followed by chapters with detailed case studies on how to handle some of the worst situations you can imagine. Each skills chapter has questions and exercises you can use by yourself, or (better yet) together as a team. And finally, we look at important issues such as keeping yourself safe and knowing your limits. Let's get started.

PART II

Tools for Defusing a Customer Crisis

CHAPTER 2

Leaning Into Criticism

HOW WOULD YOU LIKE TO LEARN an incredibly powerful technique that will stop most angry people in their tracks? It is proven, effective, and has good research behind it. And yet you probably never use it. Why? Because for most people, it feels like bungee jumping off a steep cliff. But once you take that leap, everything will change.

This technique is deceptively simple: Lean into what someone else is saying, and embrace that person's criticism—with gusto—every time he or she speaks. In other words, when flames are coming at you, walk right into them and crank the heat up even higher.

Picture this: You just flew into town for Aunt Matilda's wedding. It was great, according to everyone who went. And you have to take their word for it, because your rental car from Bonzo Rent-a-Car broke down somewhere between the airport and East Tumbleweed, and you spent the whole afternoon waiting for someone to mosey on over and fix the radiator. Now you are back at the rental-car counter. Compare these two exchanges:

You: Your rental car broke down and made me miss my family wedding, and I am furious!

Bonzo Rent-a-Car: I'm sorry, Ma'am, but unfortunately we aren't responsible for any consequential damages.

You: Your rental car broke down and made me miss my family wedding, and I am furious!

Bonzo Rent-a-Car: Of course you're furious! My goodness, this made you miss a wedding! Please tell me what happened here.

Which of these two openings is more effective? You know which one. I do not have to tell you. But you also know how most people react when a customer lights into them: They stand there with no idea what to say next, until they finally stammer something defensive that makes things even worse. Perhaps you do this yourself? (Be honest.)

Let's break this situation down. You probably feel you have two choices: (1) defend yourself or (2) respond to the complaint. (Many of us also consider a third option: run!) Most of us instinctively choose the option that is virtually guaranteed not to work, namely the first one. Customers tell us how horrible we are, human nature takes over, and we try to explain that we aren't really that horrible. Or we try to "educate" them about our policies and procedures. Or we try to tell them that we usually are much better than we were in the situation that ticked them off.

What then follows isn't a matter of attitude. It is a matter of physics. You have done the equivalent of dropping a Mentos into a bottle of cola, causing a violent eruption. The customer feels unheard, and responds the way unheard customers usually do—which is not pleasant.

This leaves us with the other option: Respond to the complaint. This works better than defending yourself, but even this doesn't always work well. Have you ever been in a situation where you felt you tried to address a customer's complaint, but the customer still got angrier and angrier?

When someone is unhappy—especially if he is really unhappy—we tend to lean away from his complaints, emotionally and sometimes physically. We give bland acknowledgments, try to minimize the problem, and make excuses. Or worse, we say nothing at all. Even our body language gives us away: We tend to back off, make less eye contact, and close up our stance.

I propose doing something very different: Throw yourself headlong into the person's grievances. Be right there with every bit of anger and indignation he is feeling. And then watch what happens. More often than not, the tension drains away, and you are suddenly in a rational conversation with Mr. Angry. That's because he now realizes that you "get" him, and all that negative energy he was going to invest in fighting you has harmlessly vaporized.

Of course, there is much more to defusing a customer crisis than leaning into the other person's emotions. At some point, you have to shift gears into problem solving. (We will talk about that a little later in this book in Chapter 6, particularly on focusing on what you *can* do.) But you will never get there unless you can show customers that you hear them, and get them on your side. In this chapter, we show you how leaning in can work effectively with a four-step process.

Step 1: Hand Their Complaints Back to Them

Imagine you are standing behind the front desk of a large hotel with a tired and angry guest in front of you. The air-conditioning didn't work in her room last night, the front desk couldn't or wouldn't do anything about it then, and now the guest is telling you what a horrible night she had. What do you say first?

This part is easy, because the customer just handed you the words. Put them in your own words, and hand them right back to her. For example, "That's terrible! It sounds like you hardly slept a wink last night." Try these other examples on for size:

Customer: You did a horrible job of painting my kitchen! I can't stand to even look at it now.

You: Yikes! It sounds like this paint job didn't work for you at all. Please tell me more about what went wrong.

Customer: Your stupid product messed up my engine.

You: Wow, so this product actually caused engine trouble—in a new car, no less! That's really scary.

Customer: What you just said to me sounded patronizing.

You: My apologies, I obviously hurt your feelings! Please tell me what bothered you about it.

In each of these cases, you took a moment to live where your customer lives instead of just jumping headfirst into your side of the story, even in the third example, where someone said something very challenging and personal to you. By taking their words and handing these complaints right back to them, you let them know that you heard them, that you processed what they were saying, and that it is safe to talk about it.

This technique is a form of *paraphrasing*, which we will discuss in more detail in the next chapter. It works best when you put the customer's complaint in your own words as much as possible. Put your personal touch on what customers are telling you, and hand their thoughts back to them respectfully as a gift.

Step 2: Use "Wow" Words

Handing back someone's complaint works even better when you use what psychologists call *mirroring* to reflect a customer's emotions. If he is agitated, respond vigorously. If he is doing a slow burn, speak deliberately and with as much gravitas as you can muster. Be right there with him, use his words and thoughts, and match him feeling for feeling.

Most of us try to minimize bad things. We grew up that way. Think about phrases like "It sounds like you have a little problem with that." "Others have had it worse." "Calm down." "You'll get over this." You probably use phrases like these yourself, because you think they will make the customer's scary monsters shrink down and go away.

Instead, they have the opposite effect. Let me translate these phrases into what customers hear: "Go away. I don't hear you. I don't care what you are saying. I'm not listening. La-la-la-la-la-la." This is why these phrases do not give you the results you want.

Instead, I want you to make a 180-degree turn in the road. Pick words that mirror the customer's feelings as she stated them, and blow them up larger than life. Meet her where she is, and then go her one better. Give these examples a try:

Customer: You almost caused a horrible accident out there!

You: You're right, that was a close call! We're lucky someone didn't get hurt or killed!

Customer: Your stupid camera didn't work at my daughter's graduation!

You: At your daughter's one and only graduation ceremony? That's *awful*! I'd be furious about that!

Customer: This food is terrible!

You: Wow! Sounds like you had a miserable lunch!

You see, your goal right now is to get the customer nodding his head up and down to whatever you say so you can calm him down and keep talking. If he doesn't think you "get" him, it becomes his sworn duty to fix that by pressing you even harder. "Wow" language is a preemptive strike that takes hearing and feeling his story completely off the table so you can both calm down and get to business.

"But wait," you say. "Doesn't using 'wow' language imply that you agree with the customer, or that the situation is your fault?" No, it doesn't. There is all the difference in the world between acknowledging someone and agreeing with that person. Even the world's heartiest acknowledgment doesn't change what happened, who is at fault, or what you will do about the situation. For now, your mission is to build a connection, and the quickest and most powerful way to do that is to match the customer's emotions.

A Tale of Two Salespeople

One day I was asked by two salespeople, within twenty-four hours, to purchase extended warranties on products I was buying. Based on experience, I would rather be pecked to death by ducks than purchase an extended warranty. So compare the following two encounters.

The first was at a chain office-supply store—the same chain that put me through three weeks of torture and paperwork a few years ago when I tried to get it to fix a broken CD drive under its extended warranty. After the salesperson pressed me a couple of times to purchase a warranty for my printer, I finally spilled my tale of woe. The salesperson responded by staring at me blankly and saying, "But we've changed suppliers since then."

The second encounter was with an appliance salesperson. When he asked me about purchasing an extended warranty, I shared the story of how another appliance store made me wait weeks before strolling on over and fixing a leaking water heater, with as much bureaucracy as could be brought to bear. This salesperson responded by stiffening up and saying, "That is totally *un*-acceptable! If I had an experience like that, I probably wouldn't want an extended warranty either!" Then he politely explained the benefits of *his* store's plan.

In the first case, I dismissed the salesperson as a clueless nitwit. I had just shared how his chain had made my life miserable the last time I listened to its song and dance, and he couldn't have cared less. In the second case, however, I was listening. I paid attention to what this salesperson had to say. And if there was any way I could have been talked into purchasing an extended warranty (there wasn't), he would have had a pretty good chance. He had my trust.

Step 3: Steal All Their Good Lines

This part is fun. Most people who serve the public worry about reactions to what they do. Instead of worrying, predict how they might react and get there first! Take a look:

- **You just wrote a parking ticket**: "Amazing. I show up and write a ticket just before you get back to your car."
- **You've run out of the hottest new Christmas toy, there are no rain checks, and a customer is livid about this**: "You probably drove all the way down here just to get this."

► **One of your students just flunked the big exam**: "What a pain in the neck for you! You were probably hoping to have this course over and done with."

I once went to my dentist hoping to get a small filling to take care of a toothache. He looked at my X-rays, turned to me, and said, "You are going to need a crown." But before I could respond, he continued, "You didn't want to hear that. You are thinking that crowns are expensive. And they take a couple of days out of your life. No fun at all. But here is why you should get one. . . ." At this point, all I could do was sit there in stunned silence, because he had taken all of my lines. (And I am now the proud owner of a new crown.) That stunned silence—the result of being heard and anticipated—is exactly the kind of outcome you want.

Step 4: Never Defend Yourself First

So far we have mentioned three things you should say. Now, here is one thing you should never say *first*: anything whatsoever to defend yourself.

Once in a great while I can read people's minds, and I can read your mind right now. You are thinking, "But what if you are right and they are wrong? What if there are consequences? What if I have good and valid reasons for what happened? Why can't I defend myself?"

Here's why: The customer isn't listening to you. Anything you say that defends yourself is going to pass through undigested at best, or enrage the customer at worst (probably the latter). In this moment, it is all about the customer. So your job is to get her listening to you first, and lay out the facts later. Here are some examples:

Customer: This is all your fault! (Note: It isn't.)

You: No one wants to feel cheated. Let's look at what happened.

Customer: Your clerk was incredibly rude to me! (Note: You overheard them both, and the customer was the one who was unreasonable.)

You: Everyone deserves to be treated with respect. What did the clerk say that offended you?

Customer: I'm upset, and I demand the moon and the stars. (Note: She won't get them.)

You: We both want to make this situation right.

Note that I did not say you can't *ever* defend yourself. At some point the facts of the matter can, and perhaps must, come out. But if you don't *first* lean into what they are saying, they have beans in their ears and cannot hear you. Defending yourself too soon is ineffective when you are right and outrageously offensive when you are wrong.

Deliver Us from Bad Service

One year the street I lived on and ran my business from was renamed. Most delivery companies figured out how to deliver to this new address. But one delivery service often circled my town cluelessly with packages from my biggest client, having no idea where to go and eventually returning them to their senders.

I tried to sort this out with the carrier repeatedly. Its toll-free number routed me to the local office, and someone there would say something like, "Oh, you must have told Patty about your new address. Patty doesn't work here anymore. Now you'll have to talk to Trixie about it."

The third time I called after missing a key delivery, the woman on the other end of the line said, "Look, sometimes we have problems with local deliveries, but at least no one can touch our international services." As luck would have it, I had just returned from teaching a training course in Montreal, where this same delivery service refused to ship back my client's computers at the last minute because its American account number didn't work in Canada, as I took great pleasure in explaining to her.

Oh, by the way, this delivery company did finally figure out how to handle my situation: It eventually ceased operations in the United States.

So what *can* you do? Hear them and learn from them. And then, of course, shift gears into problem solving, hopefully with someone who is now listening to you instead of screaming at you. That is really all there is to it. You follow exactly the same approach whether the customer is right or wrong, the consequences are large or small, or the problem is solvable or not.

Why Leaning In Is So Hard

Leaning in is simple, powerful, and it works. So why do we so often say exactly the wrong things in moments of crisis? Because our intelligence trips us up. Critical situations put us on high alert, and that wonderful brain of ours kicks into overdrive coming up with ways to protect ourselves. Here are a few of the things your intellect is pounding on the door to tell you when someone is ranting at you:

▶ **If I give credence to the complaint, it will become my fault**. Guess what: It already is your fault—in the customer's mind. That is all that matters to the customer. And your silence simply makes you all the more complicit in this situation.

It often feels strange to be emphasizing how horrible and awful something is for a customer. It almost seems like an admission of guilt to the person saying it. But to the listener, the exact opposite is true. You become someone who "gets" that other person, and the listener instinctively flips a switch that turns you from foe to friend. And that makes everything that follows much easier.

▶ **The customer might demand more than I can give**. Might? Heck, she probably will. So answer this question: What is more likely to rile up a customer into demanding too much: if you hear and acknowledge her, or if you turn into a block of ice?

Upset customers often pose, posture, and make outrageous demands. They do it when you try to help them, and they do it—a *lot* more often—when you try to ignore them. So you might as well let them do what they do, and then trust your communications skills to handle the situation.

We devote Chapter 8 of this book to what to do when people demand too much, but here is a sneak preview. When you acknowledge what another person wants, validate the feelings behind those requests, and focus on what you can do, you have a much better rate of success than if you use the "I'm sorry, sir" approach that human nature is pulling you toward.

▶ **I will just be fueling the anger by acknowledging it**. Think about a parent with a fussy three-year-old in the seat of a grocery cart. The child is screaming, crying, and demanding candy. Ignoring this behavior or changing the subject sometimes makes the firestorm pass. The child slowly learns that yelling doesn't always get you what you want, and the parent learns to turn a deaf ear to angry outbursts.

But your customer isn't three years old, and you aren't the customer's parent. By going ostrich, you commit the cardinal sin of trying to defuse conflict: You make someone who is feeling unheard feel even more unheard. He reacts by puffing himself up to be even more threatening so you will pay attention to him. See where this is heading?

You aren't alone here. Whole cultures often learned to deal with conflict by shutting down to it. We probably wouldn't have had Visigoths sacking Rome in the Middle Ages if people could have figured out how to productively address their concerns (seriously; read your history books). And even today, many of us try to ignore or minimize the problem in front of us—and then pay a steep price.

I want something much better for you: I want you to be able to confidently defuse any situation. One of the first steps toward that goal is learning that you are almost always better off responding to an upset customer with gusto, and trying to see the world as she sees it. Try it the next time a customer is upset, and watch what happens.

PUTTING LEARNING INTO PRACTICE

1. You work for a large rental company. A customer marches in and shouts, "The tent you put up for us leaked and everyone got drenched, along with their meals! You've completely ruined our son's graduation party." What is your response?

_____

_____

_____

2. The utility company you work for mistakenly sent disconnection notices to several thousand people because of a computer error, and—lucky you—you are on the phones today answering one call after another from customers who are furious about this. What is the first thing you say to each person?

_____

_____

_____

3. You are a young doctor and get a surprise visit from a patient you saw yesterday. "Look at me!" she exclaims. She is covered from head to toe in a rash caused by the medication you prescribed for her the day before. What do you say now?

_____

_____

_____

CHAPTER 3

Achieving Deep Acknowledgment

YOU DO NOT KNOW HOW to acknowledge other people. Especially difficult ones.

I mean this statement in the nicest possible way. In my experience working with groups ranging from senior executives to front-line employees, the vast majority do not know how to acknowledge a truly obnoxious, demanding customer. These are good people who try hard to do the right thing with customers, and they either struggle with what to say as they are being taunted, baited, or yelled at, or they fall back on empty catchphrases that don't work.

Now I am going to make another bold statement: Your inability to acknowledge people *causes* the vast majority of your most difficult customer situations. "Wait a minute!" you are probably thinking. "Why is it my fault when people get too emotional, have unrealistic demands, or won't accept the best that we can do?"

The reason is that more often than you think, these seemingly one-way encounters are really a dance with two partners. Here is why: Even outrageous customer behavior often calms down when it is *heard* instead of just reacted to. Conversely, it usually escalates when it isn't heard. Compare these two responses:

Customer: This is totally unacceptable!

You: Sir, let me explain how our policy works.

Customer: This is totally unacceptable!

You: I can tell by your tone of voice how annoyed you must be. No one likes to be kept waiting like you were. Let's look at some options together.

The first response may sound reasonable on paper, but it translates to customers as, "Drop dead. We don't care what you think or feel." Often, it will provoke a reaction. The second response "gets" the customer by letting her know you heard her frustration before you move to the heavy lifting of negotiating a solution. Being able to respond this way simply requires being taught new skills.

This leads me to a third bold statement: Acknowledging people is the most powerful tool you have in difficult customer situations. It is often the only way to turn anger into productive dialogue. In this chapter, we look at why most of us would rather drink poison than acknowledge others—and how we can change this.

Why We Don't Acknowledge Demanding Customers

Why is acknowledging the concerns of your worst customers so difficult? I believe it is a simple problem of linguistics: We have a mistaken idea of what the word itself means.

The roots of the word *acknowledge* date back to the fifteenth century, when it meant to give your *accord* to another person's *knowledge*. It does not mean that you are agreeing with the other person. Nor does it mean that you will give him whatever he wants. It just means that you respect his viewpoint, even if you personally disagree with it.

Because we wrongly feel that acknowledging infuriating, demanding people is the same as giving in to them, we often—with the best intentions—do the one thing that is guaranteed to never, ever work: Point out how wrong they are. We explain our policies, set boundaries, or worse, try to "educate" these customers about how their problems are their own fault. Then they predictably pose, posture, threaten us, and demand to speak to our managers.

Most crisis professionals will tell you that good acknowledgments are the easiest and most powerful way to defuse a situation while still respecting your own boundaries. Moreover, acknowledgment is a totally mechanical process. Once you learn how to do it, you can practically do it in your sleep.

The Four Powerful Levels of Response

This chapter will teach you what I call the "ladder of acknowledgment": four increasingly powerful levels of response that you can choose from in a difficult customer situation, each of which can dramatically help you defuse it. These four levels are:

1. **Paraphrasing**: Mirroring the customer's statements empathetically

2. **Observation**: Reflecting what the customer is thinking and feeling

3. **Validation**: Letting customers know their feelings are valid—at least to them

4. **Identification**: Sharing what you feel in common with the customer

By choosing one of these four approaches—paraphrasing their words, observing their thoughts and feelings, validating their concerns, or identifying with their emotions—you provide a face-saving way for difficult customers to calm down and enter into a rational, problem-solving dialogue with you. Let's look at how these four approaches work.

Paraphrasing

Paraphrasing is easy and powerful. You simply take whatever other people say, gift wrap it with your own words, and hand it right back to them. In the process, you let them know that (a) you heard them, (b) you have processed what they are saying, and (c) it is safe to talk about it.

Paraphrasing Your Way out of Trouble

One client of mine, a major state university, had a big problem: graduation audits. Students would contact the administration and say, "Hi there! I'm ready to graduate!" The school would do a lengthy audit to see if the student really was ready to graduate. Sometimes the answer was no—a student would be two credits short, or lack a distribution requirement, or something else. Often, staff members so dreaded calling students back about this that they put off doing it.

So the next time I did a presentation for the staff, I invited one brave person to come up on stage with me and role-play this situation. And she did a truly wonderful job. Shouting and pointing her finger in my face for emphasis, she exclaimed, "This is *no fair*! No one told me about any of this! And I have a job waiting in two weeks! This is *all your fault*! You have got to fix this!"

In response, I did exactly what I told the audience I would do: I simply paraphrased everything she said. Here are some of the things I said in response:

"Wow, so no one ever told you about this!"

"You've got a job in two weeks, so this is really urgent!"

"We've got to find a way to help you graduate as soon as possible!"

Her response? She stood there with a look of stunned silence on her face, thinking to herself, "Hey, wait a minute! I'm trying to get angry with this guy, in front of all these people, and *I don't know what to say*!" That's because I had addressed everything she brought up, every time she opened her mouth.

When a customer gets upset with you, and you have no idea what to say in response, paraphrasing is a great place to start because the customer is handing your response to you. Here are some techniques for doing it well:

Start with listening. Give customers the time and space to say whatever they feel they need to before you jump in with a response.

Remember, a talking customer is your friend. He or she is giving you lots of information to paraphrase, as well as the time to create a good reply.

Respond—don't editorialize. There is a time and place for your side of the story, and it isn't when you first acknowledge someone. Good paraphrasing reflects the world as the customer sees it, not as you see it. Resist all temptation to spring your own agenda on what the other person is saying. For example, when a customer says, "I think your company stinks," don't respond with, "So you think our company stinks. Here is why we're actually better than most companies." Instead, stick to the customer's agenda ("You are pretty upset with us. Tell me more.").

Put their words into your own words. One example of paraphrasing that usually fails miserably is when workers at offshore call centers (who have usually been trained by nonnative English speakers) repeat what the other person says word for word. Has the following conversation ever happened to you?

Customer: My credit card bill has a huge error!

Call center agent: I see, sir. So you are telling me that your credit card bill has a huge error. Is that correct?

Customer (with some annoyance): Umm, yes, I just told you that!

The more you put a customer's statements into your own words, the more you show how well you are listening. Practice replaying other people's statements with new words and synonyms, and watch how much better people respond.

Observation

The next step up from paraphrasing is to make an observation about what the person is probably thinking or feeling. Suppose, for instance, that an airline customer just missed the last flight of the day. Instead of just paraphrasing her words ("Wow, you just missed the last flight!"), you reflect what is on her mind ("You were probably hoping to get home tonight. How frustrating!").

Here are some examples of using observation phrases in difficult customer situations:

- "I can tell by your tone of voice that you are pretty upset about this."
- "This obviously didn't turn out the way you wanted it to."
- "I can see how important this is to you."

Here are more tips for making good observations:

Guessing is OK. It is perfectly acceptable to use your best judgment about what the other person is thinking or feeling. First of all, your hunches are almost always going to be correct. Second, even if they aren't, people generally will appreciate your honest attempt to hear them.

Don't minimize emotions. As we discussed in the previous chapter, match or exceed the other person's emotions step-by-step. Don't use phrases like "It sounds like you had a little problem here." Instead, go deep and mirror every inch of that person's frustration ("Wow, this really messed up your event!").

Plan your next step. This is true for all forms of acknowledgment, but especially observation: Don't stop there. Otherwise you risk sounding patronizing and having an encounter like this:

Customer: This meal was horrible!

You: So you weren't happy at all with your food.

Customer: Well, duh, yeah! What are you going to do about it?

In a case like this, simply adding a phrase like "Tell me what you didn't like about your meal" can help. Better yet, "What can we do to make this right?" links your acknowledgment to a problem-solving dialogue, a topic we discuss in more detail in Chapter 6.

Validation

With paraphrasing, you hand people back their words. With observation, you voice their feelings. Validation takes things a powerful step further. As the word implies, you are not only observing a customer's feelings but acknowledging that they are valid.

How do you do this? It's simple. By definition, validation always involves letting customers know that other people share these feelings as well. Let's look at some examples:

Customer: This product lasted only three months!

You: That's terrible! No one likes having a product break down that soon.

Customer: I've been on hold for nearly a half hour!

You: Wow, that was a long time! Everyone hates waiting on hold.

Customer: I can't figure out these instructions!

You: Don't feel bad. Lots of people have trouble with these assembly instructions. I can help you.

The key is to invite a big crowd into your response with phrases like "everyone," "lots of people," "nobody," "no one," or "just about anyone." Your goal is to let upset customers know that they are far from alone, and that their reactions are totally understandable. You can also personalize your comparisons by adding your own expertise into the mix. For instance, "In my experience, many people struggle with this."

Done well, validation is an extremely powerful way to get an upset customer working with you as a team. With practice, it can also become a natural way of responding to people. Among the four techniques presented here, consider making this one your default for most situations.

The Higher Purpose of Validation: Protecting People's Feelings

You can also validate feelings that are never expressed or spoken. Remember, at the beginning of this chapter, how people in groups I've worked with often don't know what to say? I don't just stand there and feel sorry for them. I actively let them know—along with the audience—that their response is normal and that this is why they are in the course. For example, I might say:

"See that look of terror on Terri's face? This is the most important thing you will learn today! [Audience laughs] But seriously, if any of you had bravely volunteered for this exercise, you would have probably reacted exactly the same way, and this is what I see with audiences all over the country. So now, let's have some fun with this and learn what to say."

Then I break the role-playing into steps and coach Terri so that she does a fantastic job and goes off the stage to a big round of applause. This way no one ever feels embarrassed, and people still want to hire me to come back and speak.

Identification

This is the highest rung on the ladder of acknowledgment: letting others know that you share how they feel, at some level. As with the other forms of acknowledgment, it does not mean that you agree with them or are giving in to them. It simply means that you can, by virtue of your common humanity, grasp how they might feel about a situation. In the process, you are creating a powerful bond with your customers.

While validation phrases talk about other people, identification phrases always involve you. Here are some examples:

- ► "That would bother me too."
- ► "If I were in that situation, I would probably react the same way."
- ► "What happened to you wouldn't have seemed fair to me either."
- ► "I can't imagine what this situation must have put you through."
- ► "Here is what happened when I tried that."

However, there are two kinds of situations when you shouldn't use identification. The first is when you honestly cannot identify with the person. For instance, if a woman tells me how difficult her pregnancy is, I can't say, "I can just imagine how that must be"—because I can't. I am the wrong gender, so I can only paraphrase, observe, or validate her feelings.

The other time you can't use identification is when customers say things that cross your boundaries. If an upset customer says he would like to shut down your business, you can't say, "Sure thing, I would like to see it shut down too!" (Sadly, I have seen employees respond this way.) Instead, you should dial all the way back to observation: "You are obviously pretty upset with us. Let's talk about it."

Used properly, identification is one of the most powerful ways to connect with a difficult customer. In particular, if someone is openly angry, you should go for this highest rung of the ladder whenever possible. And in any situation, consider using it to create a bond with your customer.

"He Is Too Crazy to Reason With!"

Most people who have worked with the public long enough can tell you stories of customers they felt were "crazy"—not just difficult, or arrogant, or angry, but truly irrational. These are customers who have complaints that make no sense, or constantly ramble off topic, or get unusually agitated. They often make those who serve them feel helpless and frustrated.

According to the U.S. National Institute of Mental Health, serious mental illness occurs in approximately 5 percent of the population, and as high as 8 percent in population subgroups such as teenagers. Many of these people live and work in the community and are consumers like the rest of us. You can connect with them more often than you might think if you use the right approach. Here are three tips:

1. **Don't challenge**. No one responds well to criticism, with or without mental illness. Telling people they make no sense usually just goads them to "explain" themselves further.

2. **Refocus the discussion**. Gently ask questions that focus on the customer rather than on the diatribe. "What could we do for you right now?" "What do you need?" "How are you doing today?" Often you will get a rational answer.

3. **Acknowledge their better selves**. When they do express a need or a legitimate feeling, acknowledge it. "Good choice." "I can see why that is important to you." "Absolutely, most people feel that way."

How do I know these techniques work? Lots of personal experience. Speaking with mentally ill people on a regular basis as a crisis-line counselor, I found that this approach often turns rambling encounters into constructive dialogue because mentally ill people are still people, and they tend to respond to human kindness like anyone else. Just like your customers will.

Acknowledgment: Your Key to Handling Any Situation

The goal with all of these techniques is to show difficult customers that you "get" them. The main reason people behave the way they do when they are upset with us is because they think it will force us to see their view of the world. When we show that we understand their view—which is not the same as agreeing with them—there is often nothing to fight about. This is why good acknowledgment is the key to defusing situations and creating real dialogue.

But let's be frank: Acknowledgment is controversial. It often feels like "kissing up" to people you totally disagree with. It certainly doesn't feel natural to most of us. This is why the vast majority of the time, most people never do it—especially in their most difficult customer situations.

Here is why I want you to move past this speed bump: Good acknowledgment is one of the most powerful skills you can develop to connect with people. When first responders like police officers and hostage negotiators face critical situations, acknowledgment is the first club out of their bag. It is how psychotherapists get sullen, withdrawn teenagers to open up and talk in a way that their parents never can. And it is how you—and your whole team—become people who can handle any customer in any situation.

PUTTING LEARNING INTO PRACTICE
----

1. A customer storms up to you and declares, "Your crew did a terrible job of landscaping on my property. See how uneven this line of shrubs is? I'm going to tell all my neighbors to stay away from your company!" How might you paraphrase what she is saying?

_____

_____

_____

2. How would you make an observation about what she is thinking and feeling?

_____

_____

_____

3. What might you say to validate her feelings?

_____

_____

_____

4. What could you say that would show her that you personally identify with her, in a way that doesn't bash your employer?

_____

_____

_____

CHAPTER 4

Avoiding Trigger Phrases

HUMAN NATURE often does something amazing for us in our most difficult customer situations: It leads us to say exactly the wrong thing—particularly in a crisis.

This is a survival instinct that dates back to when we were cave people in prehistoric times. When someone challenges us, threatens us, or makes us uncomfortable, we push back. We tell people what we can't, don't, and won't do. We lay the blame for the problem at the customers' feet. Then we make the situation even more difficult for them ("Sorry, you'll have to speak to a manager about that. And you'll have to come back next Tuesday when the manager is here."). And then customers react in ways that are not exactly pleasant.

Here is a simple example. Picture someone calling your electronics store. He is furious because the hard drive on his computer just crashed and he lost all of his files, as well as a document he was working on. He is blaming this on you and your business. And he is using some pretty choice words about it.

Now, be honest: At any point in this conversation, would you tell him that he should have backed up his data? If you even so much as hinted at this, then the verbal explosion that followed would not be just his fault. It would be yours too. If you look critically at many customer situations that go wrong, you will find a similar dynamic at work.

In this chapter, we look at how you can keep your words from steering a customer's reactions completely off the rails. We look at several common phrases that people like you and I frequently use, why you should stop using them, and, more important, what to say instead. In the process, you will learn that one of the most important principles for handling difficult customer situations is knowing what *not* to say.

The Other Golden Rule

First, let's start with a general principle for what not to say.

Most of us are familiar with the Golden Rule: Treat others the way you would want to be treated. It is a good rule as far as it goes. But I would like to introduce an even more important rule, especially for challenging customer situations. I call it the Other Golden Rule:

You can never successfully criticize anyone about anything. Ever.

You see, we often respond to difficult or angry customers by trying to hold them accountable for their behavior. We tell them what they should have done, or shouldn't have done, or what our policy requires them to do first. And then we wonder why these customers get so upset.

Most of us already know this principle in our hearts. So why do we do it anyway? Because of our old friend human nature. When people are rude, arrogant, demanding, or threatening, one of the hardest things in the world to do is say things that benefit them—and it is oh so tempting to stick it to them.

Here is why I want you to resist that temptation: Criticizing someone is the verbal equivalent of steering an aircraft into a thunderstorm. You may get through the experience, but it will be a very bumpy ride.

Ironically, many people who do this feel they are following the first Golden Rule. They feel that they would deserve to be held accountable themselves in the same situation, so they treat customers that way. But no one ever likes being on the receiving end of it. It feels like buck-passing and high-handedness to both us and our customers. Especially your most difficult ones.

Trigger Phrases and How You Can Avoid Them

Now let's look at some specific types of phrases that lead customers to feel criticized, unheard, or disrespected—and how to train yourself out of saying them.

Giving Orders

The simplest way to mess up is to order your customers around.

As a customer, I have one of the longest fuses of anyone I know. But one day I was standing in a chain sandwich shop, trying to get a better look at the menu on the wall, when one of the people behind the counter barked at me, "Stand over here to order, sir!" and pointed sharply to the other end of the counter. She did succeed in getting me to move: I walked out and never returned.

Perhaps you would never treat your customers like that. But before you dismiss a story like this as the act of an isolated nasty person, look at some other phrases that seemingly nice people use all the time with customers:

- ➤ "You'll have to . . ."
- ➤ "You should have . . ."
- ➤ "Did you . . . ?"
- ➤ "I need these three forms signed."
- ➤ "Please go to the end of the line, sir."

All of these statements have one thing in common: a distorted sense of who is serving whom. Yet most of us say them as naturally as we breathe. And then we wonder why a certain percentage of our customers act belligerent.

Of course, we all sometimes have to tell customers to do things. How do you keep this from sliding down the slippery slope into bossing them around? By choosing new words that speak to your customers' interests. Especially your most annoying ones. Here are some examples:

Not so good: I'm sorry, sir, but you'll just have to wait. You aren't the only sick person in this emergency room.

Better: We know you aren't feeling well, so we'll get you in to see someone as soon as we possibly can. I am estimating about 20 minutes right now, but please feel free to keep checking in with me.

Not so good: You should have kept your receipt to get warranty coverage.

Better: Lots of people forget to keep their receipts. Let's look at the options we have from here.

Not so good: I need these forms filled out.

Better: These forms give us permission to treat you, and also address your privacy. I'd be happy to answer any questions about them.

As a general rule, ask yourself how it will benefit a customer to do what you say, and then speak to those benefits whenever possible. (And try to avoid "negative benefits," like, "If you don't do this, something bad will happen.") With practice, you will find that almost any situation can be addressed in a positive and a negative way. Choose the positive one whenever possible, and suddenly your customers will seem a lot more reasonable.

A Tale of Two Trees

There is only one thing worse than having a huge tree fall and hit your house: having a huge tree fall and *miss* your house. That's because in the latter case, *you* have to pay to have the tree removed, instead of your insurance company. I know, because both of these situations have happened to my wife and me.

In each case, we called arborists who did a technically proficient job of removing the tree. But the first arborist spoke to us using phrases like these:

> ➤ "You're lucky that I was able to come over."

> ➤ "I've got a lot of other jobs from this storm, so you'll have to wait at least three weeks."

> ➤ "I usually don't do small homeowner jobs like this. Here's what you will need to do when we come."

Later, after the other tree fell in another storm, we called a second arborist. Here are some of the things he said to us:

> ➤ "I'm glad you called me."

> ➤ "Even though I have lots of other jobs, I know you'd like to take care of this as soon as possible. Would it be OK if I planned to handle this sometime in the next three weeks?"

> ➤ "Here's what you can expect when our crew comes over."

Notice that both people said almost exactly the same things, but the first one sounded entitled and arrogant, while the second one focused on us. He welcomed our business, proactively gave us information, and made us feel like we had choices, even when we didn't really have much choice.

Over the years we have spent thousands of dollars more with the second arborist than the first, giving him our business for routine tree care. If you run a business, you can put a lot more money in your pocket by simply changing the language you use.

Catchphrases

Quick—what is the most common reply you hear when you tell someone, "I understand"?

When I ask audiences this question, they always respond in unison: "No, you don't!" It almost seems a little unfair. Here you are trying to be sympathetic, and people are snapping back at you.

Here is the problem. You are using what is called a catchphrase.

Through overuse, catchphrases can become dulled to the point that people react negatively to them.

Take the phrase "I understand." People love to be understood. We almost never do enough to understand our customers. But when you use the catchphrase "I understand," your words carry the weight of every bored, finger-tapping clerk who has said, "Yeah, yeah, I understand," during that customer's lifetime. And then you lose.

Here are some other common types of overused catchphrases:

- "Don't worry." (If the customer didn't have a reason to worry, the customer wouldn't be bothering you.)
- "Calm down." (Do you like being told how to feel?)
- "Never mind." (Usually said in a tone of voice indicating you mind very much.)
- "Who knows?" (The customer was hoping that *you* knew.)
- "It's OK." (No it isn't.)

Finally, there is a very special type of catchphrase: "I'm sorry." Apologizing to people when necessary is very important. But the phrase "I'm sorry" is followed so frequently by the word "but" that people are practically expecting it. As a result, your well-intended apology often sounds forced and insincere.

There is an easy fix to using catchphrases: Choose different words. *Any* different words. As long as you don't trigger the catchphrase reflex, you will be fine. Instead of "I understand," tell customers that you can see how frustrated they are, or how much something inconveniences them. Instead of "I'm sorry," apologize for what happened in detail. With any catchphrase, just say something different—even if you make it up on the spot—and your customers will feel much better.

Setup Phrases

Did you know that we sometimes try to deliver bad news to customers by making it even nastier?

For instance, you say to a customer, "I hate to tell you this. . . ."

But by golly, there you are telling the customer anyway. Why did you say that? And what kind of reaction did you expect from it? (Hint: It is not usually a good one.)

This is an example of what we call a setup phrase. Setup phrases are usually said, without as much as a second thought, to prepare someone to receive bad news. Unfortunately, they never work. Examples of these phrases include:

- ▶ "Let me be honest with you. . . ." (Is anyone stopping you?)
- ▶ "I'm not sure what you were expecting." (If you really aren't sure, why aren't you asking the customer?)
- ▶ "I don't know what to tell you here." (Then quick, find someone who does!)
- ▶ "What can I say?" (How about, "What can I do to help you?")
- ▶ "With all due respect . . ." (Usually said in a tone of voice conveying no respect whatsoever.)

Each of these phrases translates to a single, common meaning: "I do not respect what you want and have no interest whatsoever in helping you." They are said in hopes of establishing that you are the one with the power and the customer is not. But customers who feel powerless erupt far more often than you would like.

By comparison, the right kind of introduction can make bad news much more palatable. We discuss how to do this in more detail in Chapter 5. In the meantime, banish setup phrases from your vocabulary, starting now. They will accomplish nothing you want and will put you at great risk of having your customers push back hard at you.

How to Tell Customers They Are Stupid—Effectively!

What do you do when a customer is so wrong that you really feel you have to say something about it? There is actually a perfectly safe way to do this, with the help of a little behavioral psychology. I call it the "I" technique. When I teach this in live workshops, I often paraphrase it as, "How to tell people they are stupid, without ever using the word *stupid* in the sentence."

You see, psychologists have long taught a principle known as modeling. It means that people do not learn most things from scratch. Instead, they learn by watching other people. Especially when those other people are messing up. So if you challenge customers, they almost always get defensive—but if you let them see someone else doing something stupid, they will learn from it. Especially if that someone else is you.

The "I" technique uses modeling to tell people what *you* have done in a way that helps them learn from your mistakes. For example, take the person at the beginning of the chapter whose hard drive crashed. Using the "I" technique, I might say, "*I* get really frustrated when *I* don't back up my data, and *I* lose all *my* work, so *I* know how you feel." The results are truly magical: People listen to me when I say things like this, and they never, ever get upset.

So what do you do when someone does something so incredibly, mind-numbingly stupid that you could never admit to doing it yourself? Simple. Just observe other people instead of yourself: "I've seen lots of people do things like that." Either way, a little modeling can help you walk safely into any teachable moment.

One-Sided Explanations

Perhaps the worst kind of wrong thing to say comes when it's all about you, and not at all about the customer.

Let's take what is perhaps the most infuriating phrase in all of customer service: "Sorry, that's our policy." Did you give the customer a vote in creating this policy? Did the customer assist you in implementing it? Was it the customer's idea? If the answer to these questions is "no," then guess what: The customer does not care about your policy and may well tell you where you can stuff it.

The same thing is true about other statements that benefit only you and not the customer. For example:

- ► "It is the end of my shift."
- ► "That would require us to do the job all over again."
- ► "We can't do that."

These statements may all be technically correct, but they are also infuriating because of what they imply: "We don't care." In each of these cases, a customer requested something, and you made it clear that your interests are everywhere but that request.

Does this mean that you cannot ever tell a customer "no"? Nope. What it does mean, however, is that you need to change your words to suit the interests of the customer. Instead of the phrases above, try these on for size:

- ► "My partner will take over for you on this. Nice working with you!"
- ► "We could fix this by doing the job over. Before we try that, I just want to explore a couple of less expensive options with you."
- ► "Here is what we can do."

The general rule here is to answer the question, "What can you do to address the customer's agenda?" And even if the answer is "not much," use language that is sympathetic to the customer's interests. Make that your policy, and you will have many fewer confrontations.

Less Is Often More

Nearly everyone who works with the public can share experiences with challenging or annoying customers. Almost none of them will ever tell you that they helped cause the problem. But rest assured, many customer reactions are triggered by things we say with the very best of intentions.

There is much more to your interactions than your words, of

course. We have all had the experience of dealing with service employees who act bored, won't take action, or speak to us in a tone of voice that could curdle milk. But more often than not, the situations that upset us the most as customers ourselves happen when someone speaks to us with the voice of a boss, a parent, or a critical teacher, and not as an ally.

Here is a simple test: If customers often become angrier when you talk to them, instead of less angry, there is a good chance your own language could use a checkup. Write down the things you normally say to customers, check them against the list of common trigger phrases in this chapter, and see what you can start cutting out of your script. When it comes to your own very worst customer service situations, you will find that what you *stop* saying is often as important as what you *do* say.

PUTTING LEARNING INTO PRACTICE

1. A customer's child is running amok in your store, pulling merchandise off the shelves and throwing it around. What do you say to the parent?

_____

_____

_____

2. A customer finally gets to the front of a line, but it turns out to be the wrong one. Now you have to tell him that he must wait in yet another long line. What can you say that won't make this person angry?

_____

_____

_____

3. A customer is angrily complaining that his new digital camera doesn't work. As he demonstrates the problem, it is clear that he is pressing the wrong button to try to turn it on. What do you first say to him?

_____

_____

_____

4. A woman is talking loudly on her cell phone in the dining room of the golf club where you work. This is against the rules of the club, and other people are complaining. How can you "educate" this person without being insulting?

_____

_____

_____

CHAPTER 5

Divide and Conquer: The Safe Way to Deliver Bad News

WHY IS IT SO HARD to give people bad news?

Perhaps it's because we were all children once. Most of us learned the hard way that unhappy consequences often followed when we said, "Dad, I have some bad news to tell you." And too often, we experience similar results as grown-ups when we say the same kinds of things to our customers. Especially when they are our most difficult customers.

So what do we do when we really must tell people things they don't want to hear? Blurt it out and then duck? Beat around the bush? Bring in a supervisor? The urge to avoid delivering bad news is so strong that some human resources professionals have been known to deliver an entire termination interview without the person realizing they had been fired! And for those of us on the front lines of customer service, it is even harder.

Psychotherapists know that the best way to expose people to bad news is gently, in stages, with lots of empathy and support. They refer to this approach as systematic desensitization. This is similar to how they help people get over fears and phobias, by easing them into diffi- cult situations. People handle bad news better when they are given the time and space to process a difficult message, and the person deliver- ing the message listens and responds well.

In this chapter, we show you how to deliver bad news to customers by dividing your message into three distinct phases: an introduction that prepares the listener to hear something important, a summary that uses an appropriate level of detail to move the customer toward a solution, and an empathetic response to anything a customer might throw back at you. This three-step process will not only make your customer feel better, but will help you walk safely and confidently into discussions that most of us dread.

Step 1: A Good Introduction That Prepares the Customer

Let's get one thing out of the way right up front: The worst thing to say first when you are delivering bad news is the bad news.

This may sound a little disingenuous. It isn't. Linguistically and emotionally, blurting out the bad news first is the equivalent of throwing a cold, dead fish in someone's face. When people feel shocked or confronted by something they were not expecting, they react with anger. And far too often, they take that anger out on you.

If there is one guiding principle to telling people things they do not want to hear, it is: Give the bad news second. Not third or fourth or fifth; that is beating around the bush. Instead, use an appropriate introduction that prepares the customer to hear something important while you position yourself as an ally.

There is no one all-purpose introduction. The exact content of your introduction will vary according to the situation you are in and its importance to the customer. Here are some examples of good ones:

▶ **The walkthrough**: Offer to explain or walk through the situation with someone. For example, if a customer's product has broken and the warranty has expired, start by briefly recapping its terms. "Let me walk you through the warranty coverage. All parts and labor are covered for ninety days, and major components are covered for one year. Since you have had this equipment for fifteen months, let's go over some other alternatives."

▶ **The acknowledgment**: Start with a customer's likely concern. For instance, if someone urgently wanted something finished on time and it is going to be late, start by acknowledging this urgency: "I realize it was very important to you to receive this on schedule, so I want to make you aware of what has happened here."

▶ **Getting serious**: Start the conversation by acknowledging the gravity of it, both to focus the customer's attention and to make the customer aware that you are about to convey something important: "I have some difficult news about our project that I need to share with you. Could we sit down somewhere to discuss this?"

In each of these cases, your introduction serves two important purposes. First, it gives the customer the time and space to prepare for hearing the bad news. Second, it shifts the focus from you, the messenger, to the issue itself, while helping the customer see you as someone who can help.

Good introductions take time and practice, but they are a critical step in defusing bad news. For example, picture someone who is rushing up to the gate of a canceled flight at the airport. Compare these two responses:

No introduction: Sorry, your flight was canceled.

Good introduction: I need to let you know about an important change in your travel plans. You were scheduled to leave on the 6:15 flight tonight, and then connect in Minneapolis. We are going to need to reschedule your flights, and I want to go over some options with you.

In the first case, there is a good chance the customer will erupt at you, perhaps wondering why she wasn't told sooner or demanding to know why the flight was canceled, or railing against your airline in general. All because of the shock value of discovering abruptly that her flight wasn't leaving. With a good introduction, there is a much better chance that cooler heads will prevail, and the two of you will engage in productive dialogue and problem solving.

Delivering the Worst Kind of News

What if the bad news you have to deliver goes far beyond a typical customer problem? People in such professions as police work, health care, or the ministry are often the "first notifiers" who need to inform people about serious situations such as a violent crime, a terminal illness, or some other tragedy.

Dr. Nancy Davis, formerly chief of counseling services for the FBI's own Employee Assistance Unit, has produced training materials, including a video, for delivering the very worst kind of news: death notifications. She outlines a process similar to what is described in this chapter: an introduction designed to prepare someone for the bad news; a frank summary that gets to the point and avoids euphemisms (for example, saying, "Your husband has died," instead of, "He didn't make it"); and, above all, presence and compassion.

As a principal narrator in the video, FBI chaplain Dennis Hayes points out that the wrong approach to delivering a death notice can significantly increase the trauma of the event. Here is some of his advice:

- ▶ Use a team approach when possible, but choose one spokesperson.

- ▶ Never deliver bad news on the doorstep of someone's home; ask permission to come inside and talk.

- ▶ Prepare the survivor by saying, "I have some disturbing news for you. Are there any family members you would like to have join us first?" Then ask the person to sit down, which allows a moment to prepare for the news.

- ▶ Once you have shared the bad news, stop talking and let the other person process what has happened. Be prepared for a range of emotional responses, do not be judgmental, and respond with compassion.

> ► Don't use platitudes, such as saying a death is "God's will," and never tell a child that he or she is now "the man or woman of the house."
>
> Adapted from Dr. Nancy Davis, "Death Notification Training Video," http://drnancydavis.com/home/death-notification-training-video

Step 2: A Proactive Summary That Moves the Customer Toward a Solution

What was the one thing you remember most about getting bad news yourself as a customer? In all likelihood, you remember a lot of stony silence from the person delivering the message. People tend to say as little as possible when they are delivering difficult news, and in the process, many of them come off like robots. This then leads many of their worst customers to get upset and try to force them to care.

There are times when silence is a good thing. For example, the previous sidebar just discussed the importance of stopping and giving people time to react when sharing tragic news such as the death of a loved one. But for less serious situations, we often have the opposite problem: We clam up and retreat to a silence that is perceived as rudeness and indifference.

In reality, most of us aren't trying to be rude at all. Instead, we are simply moving away from the pain of the situation, like a child pulling his hand away from a hot stove. But when you learn to move toward the pain, everything changes. So step two of delivering bad news is to give a proactive summary that moves the customer toward a solution.

As the name implies, a proactive summary is information you volunteer to help the customer. Good proactive summaries have two components, details and options.

Details

Details help give the situation context. More important, they show interest in the customer. And within limits, the more detail you give, the better.

Details are not the same as excuses. Most customers will stiffen up and push back if you try to defend yourself, because no one cares whether something is your fault or not; they only care about their own agenda. But when you take the time to let them know what happened, they generally appreciate it. Compare these two responses:

Not so good: I would have installed your oven today if I could have, but the delivery guy was late. Wasn't our fault.

Better: We have a team of people involved in installation like this. Today was a rare situation where one person on the team was held up somewhere else, and we couldn't make all of our deliveries. I apologize for that. Let's see what we can do to take care of this for you as soon as possible.

Options

Options are even more important. Customers, especially difficult ones, are focused on, "What's in it for me?" So ideally, your discussion will close with options that benefit the customer.

Behind this obvious statement is a less obvious truth: The act of offering options is often as important as the options themselves. People frequently hold back from saying anything because they are afraid that what they can offer won't be good enough, or that a customer will get upset. In reality, being proactive with other alternatives usually makes things much better, as long as you are frank and constructive.

Imagine that someone checks into your hotel late at night, announces that he is starving, and your only restaurant just closed. This person's only options are a dingy pizza parlor three blocks away or driving to another all-night restaurant. Compare these two responses:

Not so good: I'm sorry, sir, our restaurant just closed.

Better: Since you are starving, and our own restaurant just closed, I'd like to suggest a couple of other options. First, there is Dingy

Pizza. It is kind of a well-worn local eating place—it serves mainly pizza—but it is the closest restaurant that will still be open at this hour. If you would like a nicer place, I do have a couple of other suggestions within driving distance.

Just the fact that you are offering options serves an important purpose. It implies that the customer has a choice, and giving people choices is one of the more important ways of making bad news palatable to them. It also opens rather than closes dialogue. For example, if you tell this hungry customer, "You'll have to go somewhere else tonight," you are choosing words that shut down the discussion, and customers will often push back against that. Options, by comparison, represent the shortest path between you and a solution.

Notice also that giving a good proactive summary does not mean sugarcoating the news. In fact, as long as you acknowledge the other person, honesty is generally a good thing. It connects you and the customer, and focuses both of you on finding the best solution.

A proactive summary that provides good details and good options will set you far apart from most people who deal with the public. Think of all the times clerks have simply dumped the problem back into your lap, saying something like, "Sorry, you'll have to wait," "We're sold out," or "Your warranty expired." When you take the time to craft a detailed, helpful explanation, you make it easier for them to absorb bad news without overreacting to it.

Step 3: An Empathetic Response to the Customer's Reactions

Once you give a good introduction and a proactive summary, it is the customer's turn to respond. If you have done a good job, the customer will hopefully react to the situation and not to you personally. Either way, you are going to hear the customer's side of how your bad news affects that person.

Your reactions to these statements are the crucial final step in delivering bad news. Sadly, most of us focus on ourselves, not the customer. We say things that are defensive, minimize the consequences, or attempt to "bring the customer back to reality." And none of this ever works.

Instead, acknowledge the customer's situation and mirror the customer's emotions by responding with empathy. Then use this empathy to link the customer with the best solutions you can. Compare our usual self-focused responses with empathetic ones:

Customer: This repair is going to cost me a fortune!

Self-focused response: We try to keep the costs of these repairs reasonable. And besides, this repair will be guaranteed for two years.

Empathetic response: You're right, this is a lot of money! No one ever wants to have to replace a transmission.

Customer: I can't believe you ran out of full-size cars, and I'm going to have to squeeze into a subcompact.

Self-focused response: Unfortunately, we can't always predict the demand for rental cars. Next time, you might want to make a reservation.

Empathetic response: I don't blame you at all for being annoyed about this. I prefer big, comfortable cars myself.

Customer: Your delays have held up this entire project.

Self-focused response: Sir, you have to understand that there were a lot of factors beyond our control.

Empathetic response: Absolutely they have! I realize that you were hoping to get this project completed last month.

These self-focused responses have two things in common: They are all technically correct, and they all make you sound conceited and indifferent because you haven't responded to a single feeling the customer expressed. By contrast, the empathetic responses all mirror exactly how the customer sees the world and defuses the customer's hostility.

The reason most of us do not use empathetic responses is simple: They make us feel like we are coming dangerously close to agreeing with the complaints and will thereby get ourselves in trouble. In reality, honoring a client's perspective almost always causes less trouble, while defending ourselves or our policies usually creates more trouble. This is one case where the long way around is truly the shortest way home: Move toward your customers every time they open their mouths, and their tension will usually melt away.

Be Prepared for Anything

One day back in my corporate career, I was pulled abruptly out of a meeting by an ashen-faced technical support agent. Something terrible had just happened with one of her customers, and she wanted me to call him about it. The customer had shipped the agent his computer so she could do a complex software installation for him, and because of a communications mix-up, our IT department mistook it for one of our own incoming computers and erased everything on its hard drive.

As the agent, the customer's account manager, and I huddled in my office, we did two things to help make this call go better. First, the account manager and I shared stories about customer situations that had gone wrong for us in the past to help everyone relax. Second, I went over what I would say on the call: my introduction, a clear description of what had happened, an unequivocal apology that took ownership of the situation, good assessment questions, and a game plan for service recovery. I suggested that we all view this situation as a lab exercise for handling a difficult situation and getting through it.

As the others held their breath, I made the call, launched into my planned dialogue, and waited for the customer's response. His reply? "Ah, there was nothing important on that computer anyway. No big deal."

The other two people let their breath out once it became clear that the customer wasn't going to get angry. And I was relaxed either way because I knew exactly what I would say and do no matter how the customer responded. The moral of this story? With the right skills and preparation, you, too, can view calls like these as "another day at the office."

Most of the time, delivering bad news effectively is as simple as following these three steps. But they all take practice; good introductions, proactive summaries, and empathetic responses rarely come to us in the heat of the moment. When you create, edit, and refine statements that work best with your own difficult messages, and then teach these statements to everyone on your team, the difference in how customers react, and in how confident you feel with customers, will truly amaze you.

PUTTING LEARNING INTO PRACTICE

1. Someone is trying to return a broken laptop to your store for a refund. The screen is cracked, there is a muddy footprint on it, and it is clear that the customer caused the damage. What might be a good way to begin your response?

_____

_____

_____

2. What kind of explanation might you give about refusing him a refund?

_____

_____

_____

3. The customer responds by complaining how expensive laptops are, and wondering why a big, profitable chain like yours can't just take this computer back. How would you reply?

_____

_____

_____

4. What options might you offer this customer to try to make the best of the situation?

_____

_____

_____

CHAPTER 6

Powerful Problem Solving: Beyond "Yes We Can" and "No We Can't"

EVERY CRISIS HAS ITS ROOTS in an unsolved problem. Thus far in this book, we have focused on ways to help a difficult customer feel heard and understood. But that is not enough. At some point, the discussion must shift to the heavy lifting of solving the customer's problem.

When customers confront us, our natural instinct is often to respond with our agenda, which in turn leads them to push back with their agenda. Or we may desperately throw out solutions and hope they will accept them. Sometimes this approach works, but often it leads to frayed tempers and escalating demands.

In this chapter, we outline a better way: a systematic, four-step approach for problem solving that involves clarifying the customer's needs, framing your response around those needs, creating incentives for a mutual solution, and responding to objections. In the process, you will learn that negotiating a solution, even with a very difficult customer, has a structure you can learn and follow.

Step 1: Clarify the Other Person's Needs

Try an experiment the next time you are out shopping: Listen to customers trying to get service. Any customers, in any situations. Pay particular attention to what the people who work at the stores say in response.

The vast majority of the time, you will hear a dialogue that goes something like this:

Customer: I want X.

Employee: We can't do X. We can do Y instead.

Customer: But I want X.

Employee: Here's why we can't do X.

Most of the time, no one is being rude here. However, both parties are talking past each other. Neither is saying anything that speaks to the other's agenda. The customer focuses on what he or she wants, and the employee is locked in on what the store can (or often can't) do.

Most of the time, this dialogue works: The customer settles for Y and walks away. However, this approach is all but guaranteed to blow up in your face with your most difficult customers, and your most difficult situations, for one simple reason: The customer feels unheard. It isn't just that you can't do what the customer wants—it's that you have responded, with the best of intentions, in a way that sounds like you aren't listening and don't care.

Here is how you can short-circuit this process: Clarify what they want. Take what they want and play it right back to them:

Customer: I demand the moon and the stars.

You: Of course. You are really frustrated, and you want the moon and the stars.

Have you agreed to give this customer the moon and the stars? Not yet. Maybe not ever. But first, you have told this customer that you heard his demands, his thoughts, and his feelings.

Here you can use any or all of the acknowledgment techniques we discussed in Chapters 2 through 5. The important thing is to clarify what customers are looking for and let them hear that first. That way you score a victory no matter what happens: Whether you can grant their wishes or not, they know you heard them. Then you are ready to move on to the negotiating phase.

Step 2: Frame Your Response

Now we get to the fun part: responding with what we can or cannot do.

If the answer is yes, you can do what the customer wants, of course this part is easy. And if the customer is a reasonable person who will accept pretty much whatever you say, this part is also easy. But when you can't give difficult customers what they want, we normally take one of three common stances:

1. We simply say no to them: "I'm sorry, sir, but this is a fine restaurant. We cannot make you a hot dog."
2. We try to "educate" them about why they shouldn't want what they want: "If you had read all 15 pages of your service contract, sir, you would know that we do not cover damage caused by lightning."
3. We try to convince them the problem is somehow their fault: "Sir, you can't expect to get a full refund when you have already worn these pants for three weeks."

The result of any of these three approaches? For most people, predictable unhappiness. And with our very worst customers, you had better bring your flameproof suit. But there is another approach, which leads us to what is perhaps the cardinal principle of effective problem solving: Lead with what you *can* do, not what you *can't* do.

Take the customer's needs, think about what you can acknowledge and what you can do, and leave the word *can't* far out of the discussion.

You see, human nature always pulls us to focus on what we cannot do, so much so that it feels really funny to suggest a smaller thing we can do in response to a big customer demand. But because people process the words they hear before they process the meaning of the words, linguistics are much more important here than you realize. People respond much more positively to you when you use the language of an ally.

Here is an example with a patient who is demanding to be seen quickly by a physician:

Customer: I want this appointment as soon as possible. The waiting is killing me!

Not-so-good response: I'm afraid we are booking appointments a month from now at this point. That is the best we can do, unless we get a cancellation.

Better response: I don't blame you for not wanting to wait. I'll tell you what we can do: Even though it is about a four-week wait at this point, I would like to put you on the cancellation list to see if we can possibly get you in sooner.

See the difference language makes? In the first case, you are handing the patient a challenge; in the second, a small victory. More important, you are packaging the same outcome in a way that honors the interests of the customer.

Here is an easy-to-remember template for framing your solution around a customer's need: "Because you [insert the customer's agenda, whatever it is], I [insert what you can do, whatever it is]."

This language links what the customer wants to what you can provide. Make no mistake, the solution you offer is very important. At the same time, the act of linking this solution to the customer is often equally important. Compare these responses:

Customer: My flights have been delayed all afternoon. I demand an upgrade to first class!

Not-so-good response: I'm sorry, ma'am. Lots of people are in your situation today. You are still going to have to stand by like everyone else.

Better response: Because you had such a bad experience, I'm going to put you on the standby list for an upgrade.

Every difficult customer, and every difficult customer situation, ultimately has its roots in an agenda. This agenda may be spoken or unspoken. It may be reasonable or unreasonable. Either way, once you learn to understand the agenda, acknowledge it, and honor it in your response, you have your very best chance of solving things peacefully.

Yes, We Can Do the Impossible—for a Fee!

One of the great things about managing a call center is the ability to monitor phone calls and see how people are doing. One day, I listened in on a really tough call. A man had never been trained to use our complex software, and as a result he had made a mistake that was going to cost him hours of extra work to fix.

He was not happy about this. In fact, he felt that this was somehow our fault and was demanding that we fly someone to Chicago the next day to "fix everything." When the agent handling the call politely tried to defer this, the customer demanded to speak with his boss—me. And I was more than happy to oblige, because it was a good learning moment for how to negotiate with a demanding but utterly wrong customer. Here were the three steps I followed:

1. **Offer to help**. I did not start with a defensive posture. Rather, I opened the conversation by politely using his name and asking what I could do to help him.

2. **Focus on possibilities**. When he predictably complained about our software and demanded that we fly someone to Chicago, I immediately replied, "We would be happy to do that for you. You should be aware that there is a lead time of three weeks for a site visit, and it costs

about $3,000." When he retorted that he did not want to spend $3,000, I was right there with him again. "Of course you don't want to spend that kind of money. So let's see what we can do to help you for free, right here on the phone."

3. **Sell the benefits.** I did not tell this person that he should have gotten training—even though I would be completely right in saying so. That would accomplish nothing but tick off an already angry person. Instead, I focused on what a training intervention would do for him, now that he was already using our system, and he listened.

The results? I never said no to him. I never criticized him for being untrained. I did not fly anyone to Chicago. And my team got to observe a good example of defusing a very demanding customer.

Step 3: Create Incentives

Perhaps the most important step of the problem-solving process is to take your best solution and make it as attractive as possible for the customer. This will give you your very best chance of having this individual leave peacefully—and, hopefully, satisfied.

You may be thinking, "This is all well and good if you can somehow still make the customer happy. But what if your only options are not going to make that person happy at all?"

Let's look at a friend of mine who was a campus police officer. One of her jobs was to take rowdy patrons at sporting events and kick them out of the arena. Not a lot of happiness there, right? But she could do it skillfully (and peacefully) by framing the situation as one that would still benefit the other person. Here is how she did it:

"Look, I know you're here to have a good time. However, I am going to need you to leave for yelling obscenities. If you leave willingly you'll preserve your dignity and be able to come back and enjoy games in the future. I would much prefer that over having you arrested and banned for the season. OK? Why don't we walk out together and make it a good night."

Now, hopefully, your own negotiations don't involve asking people to leave with a Taser at the ready. But you can still do exactly what my friend did: Create an incentive for the other person to accept your solution. Here are some ways you can make this happen in your customer service situations:

Let Them Know They Are OK

If cops can make lawbreakers feel like reasonable people, you can do the same thing with your most demanding customers. Acknowledge the fact that most of us want whatever we can get, and want situations to go in our favor, and the other person is much more likely to listen to you. For instance: "Everyone wants the best deal possible."

Contrast the Alternatives

Difficult customers often have a mindset that if they don't get exactly what they had in mind, they won't "win." So your job here is to frame your best solution as the one that will help them the most. For example, "This discount is better than what we usually offer people."

Paint a Better Future

Link your solution to a better experience in the future, and it will feel more like a victory to the customer. For example, "Next time you come to our restaurant, we can work with you to create a meal you will like better."

At the end of the day, all of us want to feel like it is all about us. Frame your solutions in terms of WIIFM—what's in it for me—and they will be much more likely to succeed.

Step 4: Respond to Objections

What happens when you acknowledge what customers want, make your very best offer, frame it to their interests—and they reply that it is totally unacceptable?

It would be delightful if upset customers would always simply accept what we propose and then walk away peacefully. Unfortunately, it does not always work that way. This is why they are difficult customers, right?

When customers object to our best offer, too many of us make a critical mistake: We start defending ourselves, restating our policies, or telling people why they should feel differently. All of these approaches have precisely the same effect: They make the customer even angrier.

Instead, continue to live where they live. Play their objections back to them. Hear them. Feel them. Accept how important they are for them. Then use these two transitional phrases to bring them back to earth: "I wish . . ." and "Even though . . ." For example:

"I realize you wanted to have this replaced for free. I wish I could do that. Even though I can't, I am still willing to offer you a discount."

These phrases move the conversation back from their problems to your solutions and offer customers at least a small victory while still maintaining your boundaries.

From there, a simple technique will often bring this standoff to a close. As you patiently acknowledge the customer's dissatisfaction and restate your best offer, be prepared to repeat this three times. After pushing back twice against your offer, a customer will usually realize by the third time that you are serious and stop pushing. So keep your cool, patiently restate your position three times, and most of these situations will be resolved.

A New Way to Solve Problems

You may not realize you are doing this, but the vast majority of the time, most of us respond to pressure and unrealistic demands by trying to somehow paint the customer as "wrong." Here, we propose a very different approach for solving problems: Accept the customer's perspective, and then use language that approaches what the customer wants as best you can. This strategy gives you your very best chance of resolving the problem while keeping your boundaries intact.

If simply changing a few words could substantially lower the amount of pressure you feel, and the level of concessions you eventually make, would you do it? When you offer solution-focused responses that show you hear customers and want to do the best you can for them, they are much more likely to accept your solutions. Try it, and the process of negotiation will seem much less onerous to you.

PUTTING LEARNING INTO PRACTICE

1. Your valet parking attendant just dented a customer's expensive car. The owner is demanding a brand new car, claiming that you "ruined" it and that it will never be right again. How do you respond?

_____

_____

_____

2. A customer is complaining that he and his family were forced to sit in front of several loud, drunken fans at your ballpark, and is demanding a refund of everyone's tickets. You have a no-refund policy. What would you say in response to his demands for a refund?

_____

_____

_____

3. Someone insists on cutting ahead of a long line because she is in a rush. What could you say to her?

_____

_____

_____

4. A young man was ordered to leave your store after shouting and cursing at your employees when he was refused a refund. Now his mother, who has only heard his side of the story, has come in demanding a formal apology. How might you first address her?

_____

_____

_____

CHAPTER 7

Reframing Your Message

WHAT IS THE DIFFERENCE BETWEEN, "I'm sorry, sir, you'll have to hold to speak to someone," and, "I can connect you to the right person, and it should be just a short wait"? Words, and nothing more. More often than you think, when a customer situation goes south, the reasons are often as simple as the words you chose.

When customers are not happy, language is often the sugar that helps the medicine taste better. Used properly, the right words can make situations sound reasonable, options seem more palatable, and warring parties become allies. They can encapsulate good intentions and customer benefits. Above all, they can calm people down.

In this chapter, we explore the art and science of reframing: choosing words that defuse situations and make solutions more attractive. Good reframing is not disingenuous, like the real estate agent who describes a small, dumpy apartment as "cozy." Rather, it puts situations in a context that helps people make rational and often face-saving choices, particularly in a customer crisis. Here we will explore the good and bad uses of reframing, and how to use it for common difficult customer situations.

How Reframing Works

In the United States, most people would rather call just about anyone but the Internal Revenue Service. So when, after filing my tax return one year, I discovered I had made a mistake on it, I was not happy about contacting them. But when I did, the agent said something that put me immediately at ease: "Yes, this is an error, and you will probably have to file an amended return and pay a small penalty. But it won't be a life-changing situation. You'll be fine."

Small penalty. Not life-changing. I'll be fine. These thoughtfully chosen words added context to a scary situation in a way that calmed me down. They sounded infinitely better than scary-sounding words like, "We will need to investigate this error and determine its seriousness." Above all, they motivated me to fix my mistake and pay my proper taxes without argument.

This is the essence of reframing: using language to increase positive emotions and decrease negative ones. Marriage and family therapists, who originally coined the term decades ago, use reframing as an integral part of therapy. They use it to make it easier for people to talk about scary feelings, open up to each other, and grow and change. Think, for example, of a couple who are always arguing. A good therapist would frame this as a sign that they both care about what they are discussing and would work with that.

With customers, reframing can be used to lessen the impact of an unpleasant situation, make the customer feel better, or make your solutions more palatable. Here are some examples:

Not-so-good response: You will have to pay a penalty because your payment was late.

Better response: There is a small fee for payments that arrive after the fifteenth of the month.

Not-so-good response: You shouldn't have parked here. It is a no-parking zone.

Better response: People often try to park here without reading the signs. Let me show you the closest place where you can park legally.

Not-so-good response: We can't get you on a connecting flight until tomorrow.

Better response: We can put you on an overnight connection that will get you home twelve hours from now.

In each of these cases, you aren't simply sugarcoating the news (that is, minimizing it in a way that the customer can easily see through). Rather, you are framing these situations around the customer's interests in a way that makes them easier to accept. The key difference is that reframing is primarily intended to benefit the customer rather than to talk the customer into something.

So how do you reframe things yourself, particularly in the middle of a developing customer situation? There are three key principles behind the mechanics of reframing.

Normalizing

This term, originally used in mathematics, means to compare things to a norm. With customers, it means describing a situation that is unusual for them as being more common or normal than they think. Here are some examples:

> *Situation*: A customer's luggage is lost.
> *Normalized situation*: "Bags often get delayed, and they almost
>   always show up within twenty-four hours."

> *Situation*: A customer is clueless about how to use a computer.
> *Normalized situation*: "Lots of people find it intimidating to use a
>   computer for the first time. We have some good resources
>   for people who are just getting started."

> *Situation*: A customer is behaving disruptively.
> *Normalized situation*: "People often get upset when things like
>   this happen. I would like to help you. Can we talk about this?"

Relative Value

This form of reframing revolves around using words to make a situation sound better. Here a delay becomes a short wait, a week becomes seven days, and a fine becomes a small fee. This works best when the comparison is credible (you don't, for example, want to call a two-month wait "short") and the intention is to make the customer feel better.

Context Framing

Here, you are putting things in a broader context to make them sound better, such as how you normally handle this situation, what a customer can expect, or what you can do. For instance:

Situation: Your hospital is running at capacity, and there is a wait for beds.

Context framing: "Our normal time frame for admitting your mother during peak periods like this should be about four to six hours. Here is what we can do to make her comfortable in the meantime."

Situation: A customer is upset because she just flunked her driving examination.

Context framing: "When people need to take the exam over, we can reschedule it as soon as a week later."

Situation: Someone who just checked in at your hotel is afraid to use the elevator, you are booked solid, and the guest's room is on the tenth floor.

Context framing: "We often send a bellman to ride with people who don't like being alone on elevators. Would you like to have me call for someone?"

In each of these cases, things work best when you prepare in advance for how you describe your most common situations. Either way, when you try to see things through the eyes of customers, you can often find a hook that gives them hope, saves face, or helps them feel understood. If you do it well, you can often make a real change in a customer's perceptions with the words you choose.

How to See People Differently? Take a Seat

You can also reframe your own perceptions of customers themselves, using a simple technique from psychotherapy. The "empty chair" technique, a fundamental part of Gestalt therapy, is used to help people develop insight and perspective about other people. Here is how it works:

> ➤ First, sit across from an empty chair. Imagine that a person you don't like, such as one of your most frustrating customers, is sitting in this chair.

> ➤ Tell the person in the empty chair exactly what you are thinking about him or her. Don't hold anything back.

> ➤ Now get up, sit in the empty chair, and respond as you imagine the other person would respond.

Amazing things can happen when you physically and verbally take on other people's perspectives. You may see their pains, their frustrations, their sides of the story. More important, you learn to describe those people in their voice, using their language. For example, someone you call a "control freak" becomes detail-oriented, a "drama queen" is someone who is often anxious and in need of reassurance, and a "hostile jerk" suddenly turns into someone who may feel voiceless, powerless, or concerned about how his children are being treated.

After you do this exercise (which you can easily do in your head), start using the other person's language to describe her and think about her in the future. Then see what it does for your own ability to engage people in productive dialogue and problem solving.

When Reframing Is a Bad Idea

As powerful as it is, reframing must be used with caution. Why? Because there is often a thin line between making a difficult customer feel better and BS-ing that person. As a general rule, this approach can be very useful as long as you don't push it too far.

Perhaps the most important tool in reframing properly is your gut. Listen to what you say through the ears of your customers—especially difficult ones—and then think through how they would react. Here are three situations you need to avoid when reframing:

Sounding Insincere

A little reframing is almost always socially acceptable, but too much of it can make you look foolish. For instance, trying to make an outrageously long delay seem normal, or a particularly bad service experience seem common, can make you seem out of touch instead of helpful.

Minimizing the Customer's Concerns

As a rule, reframing is meant to minimize your agenda, not the customer's. So although it is OK to, say, refer to stupid customer behavior as "a common situation," or your penalties as "a small surcharge," you should never refer to a customer's stated concerns as "a minor inconvenience" or a "slight problem." (In fact, as we discussed in Chapter 2, it is usually best to lean into customers' agendas and mirror their emotions.)

Being Untruthful

When reframing crosses the line from optimism to dishonesty, you risk losing the trust of your customer—or losing your customer, period.

Ultimately, reframing is a lot like acting: It works best when people are not explicitly aware you are doing it. Using gentle, nonthreatening, benefit-oriented speech will normally help you as long as you keep it within appropriate boundaries. In time, the habit of using these patterns of speaking can become an easy and natural part of who you are.

Our Client Caused an Accident? Get in Line

Once I was involved in a serious auto accident. I was stopped at a red light, in my brand new car, when a large truck plowed into the back of my car without stopping. Thankfully, I was not hurt badly, but it was a frightening experience.

A couple of hours later I was sitting in an auto body repair shop with a splitting headache and my new car crumpled like an accordion, talking on my cell phone with the truck driver's insurance company. When I finally got through to the claims department, the snippy person on the other end of the line said something like this:

"Sir, you have to understand that we have a large backlog of people with claims, and they all want their cars fixed as badly as you do. You are going to have to wait at least three days before anyone can get back to you about this."

It is a good thing I specialize in strength-based communications, because I was pretty close to saying some not-very-strength-based things in response! But what really struck me in hindsight was how unnecessary this person's whole attitude was. Suppose she said:

"I am so sorry to hear that you have been in an accident. How are you doing now? Obviously you want your car fixed as soon as possible, so I am going to personally make sure that someone gets back in touch with you within seventy-two hours." (Note: Seventy-two hours is the same thing as three days.)

By simply changing a few words around, this person would probably experience a lot less hostility from customers.

A New Perspective

Used well, reframing does much more than make difficult customers feel better; it helps *you* see a situation differently. It focuses you on solutions and lets you view customers through the same lenses they use. And like any communications skill, it gets better with practice.

Start using it as one of your regular tools and see how much it improves your customer work.

PUTTING LEARNING INTO PRACTICE

1. You are going to arrive much later than expected for a plumbing appointment. You know from experience that this customer gets upset about everything. What could you say to lessen the intensity of his reaction?

_____

_____

_____

2. A season ticket holder of the professional football team you work for is being informed that his seats are being moved to a less desirable section so more luxury boxes can be built at your stadium. How would you deliver this news?

_____

_____

_____

3. You are telling one of the patients at your clinic that she has been reported to a credit bureau for not paying her bill on time. How would you word this?

_____

_____

_____

4. A customer is extremely loud and abrasive as she describes a haircut she felt went badly at your salon. Your manager hears this and rushes over. How would you explain the situation to the manager?

_____

_____

_____

CHAPTER 8

Grounding an Angry Outburst

ANGER IS ONE OF OUR most powerful emotions. It is part of our survival instincts to defend ourselves and our loved ones against harm. But when a customer uses anger against you, it is one of the most uncomfortable experiences you will ever encounter in serving the public. It is also a nearly universal experience in customer service. Each and every one of us has probably been an angry customer ourselves at some point, and if you serve customers long enough, some of them will be angry with you too. Yet it happens rarely enough that we are often completely unprepared for it, and this in turn leads us to respond counterproductively.

No one likes to be on the receiving end of an angry outburst. But anger can be understood and managed in ways that ground its negative energy and move both parties toward productive dialogue. In this chapter, we outline a three-step process for lowering the heat: (1) choosing the highest level of acknowledgment possible, (2) asking assessment questions that "move toward the pain," and (3) shifting the discussion from blame to problem solving. Learn these steps and you will have much more control in your very worst customer service situations.

Understanding Customer Anger

Many years ago, as I was wrapping up a training course with my own call-center team, one agent described a customer who was so rude and foulmouthed that she had actually reduced a couple of our employees to tears. Then, in one of the great ironies of my career, this same customer called in the middle of this conversation. I bravely offered to take the call, and soon people were gathered around my cubicle watching Mr. Customer Service Training gasping for air under a torrent of abusive language that would make a sailor blush.

This was not a comfortable situation for me. It probably would not have been comfortable for you either. Yet because I knew what to say and what to do in these situations, within five minutes the customer and I were talking rationally, and within ten minutes we left the call as friends.

What happened in this call was typical of an interaction with a very angry customer. She came into the transaction extremely frustrated and felt that the only way she would get what she wanted was to intimidate me. So she started out by letting me have it with both barrels.

At this point, most people would react by treating this person as an enemy to be contained. They would set boundaries, tell the customer to calm down, or perhaps not react at all. The customer would then probably ramp up the assault, and the dance would continue until both parties were exhausted and upset. This transaction would likely end with one person winning and the other person losing.

This approach usually creates exactly the opposite reactions from what you want. When a customer's anger triggers a negative reaction from you, the customer attacks even harder to make sure you "get it." If such customers eventually win, they learn that this kind of behavior works. If they lose, they probably believe they should have stood their ground even more.

In my case, I responded the way I am about to teach you. I let her know that I was hearing both the situation and her anger. I did not judge her or her behavior. I asked questions designed to gather information and calm her down at the same time. Then I framed possible solutions around what she was looking for. As we went through this process, the customer's mood changed progressively from upset to civil and productive, and we eventually reached a solution that let both of us win.

This is the kind of outcome I want you to have with *your* worst customers. It was the result of a planned performance that worked as expected. Let's look at the steps that go into this performance and see how to put it to work with your own angry customers.

Step 1: Use the Highest Acknowledgment Level Possible

In Chapter 3, we talked about the "ladder of acknowledgment" and its four levels: paraphrasing, observation, validation, and identification. Most of the time, different customers and situations call for different levels of acknowledgment.

When a customer is enraged, however, this logic goes completely out the window. There are many reasons why customers are unhappy, but only one reason they become angry: They do not feel heard. They feel voiceless and powerless, and respond by puffing themselves up and confronting you until you pay attention to them. So you must head straight for the highest level of the ladder you can: Either identify with them or at the very least validate them.

This means that the first step in calming down upset customers is likely the very last thing you feel like doing: acknowledging them as deeply and with as much gusto as possible. Here's an example:

Customer: I am absolutely furious with this stupid product! This is the third time it has broken down and I have had to come back! What is the matter with you people?

Not-so-good response (defensive): Please calm down, sir!

Not-so-good response (paraphrasing): So your product broke down again.

Not-so-good response (observation): I can see you are very angry.

Better response (identification): Wow, three times! That would bother me too! Let's take a closer look at this.

Customer: I tried to get a refund on this, and your clerk was so rude to me! I am really upset right now.

Not-so-good response (defensive): Well, ma'am, we do have a no-refund policy.

Not-so-good response (paraphrasing): So you weren't happy about the way you were treated.

Not-so-good response (observation): This obviously bothered you.

Better response (validation): No one wants to feel disrespected, so I am really glad you are letting me know. Please tell me more about what happened.

See what a difference your response can make here? Here, your level of acknowledgment (identification or validation), your language (responding in detail), and your tone (matching the customer's level of urgency) all play a role in creating an effective response. Be right there with the customers in their anger, no matter how much you agree or disagree with them, and watch most of these situations start to calm down.

Finally, do not underestimate the impact of your own feelings at this stage. Anger from customers often feels frightening and inappropriate, particularly if they start out angry with no provocation from you. Every fiber of your being will want to withdraw, fight back, or defend yourself. And each of these self-protective behaviors will only make the other person angrier. Your best defense? Learn and practice what to say long before your next angry encounter, so that the right words will be there when you need them.

The Vengeful Customer

After a dealer failed to fix his expensive imported sports car—reportedly damaging it further in the process—a man in China subsequently felt he received no satisfaction from either the dealer or the car's manufacturer. So he decided to take his frustrations out in public. In front of a large crowd, with news cameras rolling to capture the event, a hired crew of men in blue jumpsuits took sledgehammers to the car and destroyed it.

He is far from alone. A 2011 *New York Times* article described someone who wasn't happy about his wedding photographers' missing the last fifteen minutes of his ceremony and, according to this customer, yelling at him when he called to complain about it. So he sued the photographers to re-create the entire wedding ceremony, at a cost of $48,000—despite the fact that he and his bride are now long divorced. And even if these photographers win in court, they have lost: Their legal bills have now topped $50,000, more than they would have paid to settle the suit.

These are examples of people who flip the switch from being unhappy customers to being vengeful ones. Others express their displeasure by creating anti-corporate websites or viral videos on YouTube, or by launching class-action suits. Many businesses dismiss these customers as simply being unappeasable. But it is rarely the case that you have no control over their existence. Here are some common denominators you will often find among customers who fight back:

▶ **They are reacting—sometimes overreacting—to a legitimate grievance**. One elderly woman became a folk hero of sorts by going to her cable company and smashing its office equipment with a hammer. This wasn't a case of someone forgetting to take her Prozac; she had repeatedly gotten nowhere requesting service and decided to take matters into her own hands. And she was more than happy to be interviewed about it afterward.

▶ **You humiliated them**. Most actions have an equal or greater reaction. When one social networking site banned a prominent blogger for twenty-four hours after she innocuously posted a picture that violated one of the site's terms of service, she responded with a video of how unreachable and bureaucratic this site was for all five thousand of her fans to see.

▶ **You simply didn't care**. One professor had a bad flight experience on a long international trip. He repeatedly contacted the airline to complain and eventually received a response the airline itself later acknowledged was "slow, impersonal and insufficiently candid." He respondedby starting a consumer website that aired grievances about this airline. It has existed for over fifteen years and gets up to thirty thousand hits per month.

So how do you prevent customers from taking public action against you? Here are some of the most important steps:

▶ **Do the right thing first**. Look at your business through the eyes of your customers. If you have poor quality, insufficient redress for problems, or labyrinthine refund policies, then your most difficult customers will react the way you or I might—only more so.

▶ **Drop the insincere corporatespeak**. If you reply to customers with stilted prose written by your lawyers or bean counters, such as, "We regret that we are unable to offer you a refund," then vengeful customers are not a random accident—they are a likely occurrence. Be open, honest, and informal about your boundaries and the reasons for them, and most people will respect you.

▶ **Reach out to your critics**. Provide solutions, or at least face-saving alternatives. Far too often, vengeful customers are reacting to being ignored as much as they are to being wronged.

Step 2: Ask Assessment Questions

Think about the last time you dealt with the police. Hopefully not in handcuffs, but rather the last time you suffered a break-in or auto accident, or needed some other kind of assistance. What do you remember most about that encounter?

When I ask audiences this question, most reply that the officer did a good job of calming everyone down. At the same time, most never really stopped to notice *how* they did this. The answer is that the officer probably did something good officers are trained to do: Ask good questions.

Good questions help turn an emotional situation into a factual one. They are particularly powerful in situations with upset customers because they move you toward the customer's pain in a way that calms the customer down. Most important, it is a necessary next step toward troubleshooting the issue and shifting the discussion to problem solving.

So when are you ready to stop acknowledging someone and start asking good questions? As soon as the heat starts to drop, even a tiny bit. If you have ever been in a situation where you felt you did everything but stand on your head to help a customer who just got angrier, chances are very good that you did not acknowledge that person enough.

What are good questions to ask? Anything that moves you and the customer toward a solution. And what are bad questions to ask? Anything that challenges the customer or sounds insincere. Here are some general guidelines.

Take a Learning Posture

People often feel that their job with difficult customers is to challenge the customers' perceptions. We ask them questions designed to convince them that they didn't read our directions, follow our rules, or remember our policies. But to calm people down, you need to turn this objective around 180 degrees and try to learn from them. Here are some examples:

- *(Customer feels your product stinks.)* "Sounds like you had a terrible experience. What kinds of things fell short for you with this product?"

- *(Customer is furious after waiting on hold for a half hour.)* "That is a really long time! How did you get treated once you finally got through? Were we able to take care of the problem?"

- *(Customer is upset with how she was spoken to.)* "I am so glad you are sharing this with me. No one wants to feel talked down to. Would you be comfortable with sharing exactly what our person said that made you feel disrespected?"

Ask them things like how they experienced the situation, what they tried to do first, and what they feel should have happened. You are not judging or agreeing at this stage—just putting yourself in their shoes and gathering information.

Never Ask "Why?"

Questions that begin with "Why" are not really questions: They are confrontations with question marks at the end of them. They never favor the customer and never move you closer to a solution. Never ask upset customers why they did or did not do something; instead, explore how they feel and what they want.

Get Specific

The best questions gather data that move you toward a solution while showing interest in the situation. This means that details are your friend. When did this happen? How long were they waiting? What kinds of things happened when they first tried to get help? The more you know, the better. And the more you can respond appropriately to this information ("Wow, that was a long wait"), better yet.

A more subtle point about good questions is that they put time and space between you and the customer's anger, allowing both sides to calm down and negotiate a solution. Don't just ask questions for the sake of asking them—people can see through that. Good questions, however, can be one of the best weapons in your arsenal for defusing a bad situation.

Step 3: Shift the Discussion

Once you have acknowledged someone enough for the heat to drop, and asked good questions to clarify the customer's position, you can now try to shift the discussion from anger to constructive problem solving.

Here you follow the same process outlined in Chapter 6: Clarify what they want, respond with what you can do rather than what you can't do, create incentives for accepting your solution, and respond to their objections. Here is an example of how this might play out with a very angry customer, including the earlier steps of acknowledging and asking good questions:

Customer: Tonight was our twenty-fifth anniversary, and this was the most horrible meal we have ever had! The waiter was rude, the food was cold, and it took more than an hour to serve us. We are beyond upset right now.

You: *(acknowledgment and good questions)* Wow! I can't believe that so many things went wrong for you on such a special occasion. I feel terrible about this, and I really appreciate your letting me know. Could you tell me what you both ordered?

Customer: I had the porterhouse steak, and my wife had chicken cordon bleu. My steak was practically raw, and her chicken was so cold that the cheese inside wasn't even melted.

You: That is horrible! I am also concerned about how the waiter treated you. Would you be comfortable sharing what went wrong there?

Customer: You bet. When I confronted him about our dinners, he muttered something about a new cook and disappeared on us. Then when he came back and we asked him to take these dinners off the bill, he had a bad attitude and told us we would have to talk to the manager. So here we are.

You: *(assess what they want)* It sounds like practically nothing went right here tonight, and on your twenty-fifth anniversary no less. What could we do to make this right for you?

Customer: I'll be totally honest. This has ruined such an important special occasion, I am thinking of seeking compensation in small claims court and letting the local newspaper's food reporter know about this as well. I feel you people should be out of business.

You: *(acknowledge and respond with what you can do)* If this were my twenty-fifth anniversary, I would be that angry too. You have the right to do whatever you feel you need to do. But since my name is on this restaurant, I would love the chance to try again and give you both the kind of evening you were planning on.

Customer: Well, you didn't do a very good job this time. Plus I'm probably getting your whole staff in trouble here.

You: *(respond to objections and create incentives)* Absolutely, we did fall down tonight, and I want to apologize to both of you for that. And of course I am going to talk to our team. Don't worry, no heads are going to roll, but moments like these help me teach people how to do things the right way. So here is my proposal. Forget tonight's bill. Pick another date sometime this month, call me personally, and let us try again to create a very special evening for the two of you. It will be on the house, and it will be our pleasure.

Customer: All right, then. We'll think about it. Thank you for listening to us.

A lot of important things went on in this discussion. First, the customer's anger was heard and acknowledged. Second, the restaurant owner showed an interest in the specifics of what happened. Third, the owner focused on a solution. But what is just as important is what didn't happen in this discussion: There were no excuses, and there was no defensiveness or pushback, even when the customer threatened the manager. This manager avoided all of these things precisely because none of it would have worked.

This is the heart and soul of defusing a difficult conflict. Keep your focus on the customer, find the core of reasonableness in the customer's frustration, and work with the customer to co-create a satisfactory solution. In this case, the manager has probably prevented a court date and lots of bad publicity for the price of a couple of dinners. And in the general case, skills like these will help you walk safely into—and out of—your worst customer service situations.

Your Secret Weapon: The LPFSA

When you are trying to keep someone from becoming upset and you have few options to work with, one tool will often save the day: the LPFSA.

The what?

The LPFSA: the Low Probability Face-Saving Alternative. It is an option you offer the customer that (1) has a low probability of being successful, but (2) addresses the customer's agenda and allows him or her to save face.

Does this sound disingenuous to you—or to the customer? Not as much as you might think, as long as you frankly inform the customer of its low probability up front.

A perfect example of the LPFSA came up a few years ago when I went to a major league baseball park during a business trip. It was a perfect Sunday afternoon: sunny, 70 degrees, Father's Day weekend, and the home team was a game out of first place. I did not know it as I pulled into the parking lot, but the game was sold out. Here is what I was told when I went up to the ticket window:

"It's a beautiful day for baseball, and we would love to see you get into the game today. Even though we are completely sold out, here is what we would like to suggest. Our season ticket holders have a tradition of dropping off extra tickets they aren't using at the gates, and if we have any, we give these away for free. I can't make any guarantees, especially this close to game time, but if you don't mind checking the other gates, it would be great if we could still get you in."

I checked at each gate: no extra tickets, but everyone was as polite and helpful as the person at the ticket window. Eventually it struck me: I had just spent twenty minutes circumnavigating the ballpark, a distance of several city blocks. I had no ticket to the game. I was walking back to my car. And largely because of how I was treated (and, I found out later, how this team's employees were trained), I was not feeling the least bit unhappy!

Here are some other examples of an LPFSA in action:

► The doctor is booked solid, but you put patients on a list for an earlier appointment if someone cancels.

► Someone gets a parking ticket, and you offer the option of appealing it by mail.

► You offer to refer a situation to your manager for a decision.

Used properly, the LPFSA gives customers something of value for their efforts—the hope of a possible solution. More important, it allows you to use the language of an ally to calm them down.

Working in the Red Zone

Our natural reaction to a customer's fury is to become frightened and defensive. I want you to have a different reaction: confidence. When you learn and use skills like these, you can truly defuse angry customer situations with the skill of a bomb squad. This confidence, in turn, will almost always carry over to your customer.

At the same time, know your limits. Communicating well in the face of customer rage takes practice. You should also be aware that the gravity of some situations will overwhelm even your best communications skills. For example, if I were to rush to the hospital after learning my wife was in an accident and was told that I would have to wait for visiting hours, there is nothing anyone could say that would keep me—or most of us—from getting angry. There is no shame in calling for help when you need it.

Chapter 19 examines what to do when situations truly start getting out of hand. It covers important techniques ranging from calling for backup to keeping yourself safe. But with the right skills, most of us need never get to that point. Anger is something you and your entire team can learn from, work with, and master—and when you do, the benefits for you, your customers, and your career are incredible.

PUTTING LEARNING INTO PRACTICE

1. You are a hospital administrator, and a mother is furious about her son's treatment: the delays, the pain, the lack of communication. How should you respond?

_____

_____

_____

2. One of your home-remodeling clients calls, enraged that your crew accidentally shattered a prized stained glass window at her house. This situation was totally your fault. How do you respond?

_____

_____

_____

3. A woman is very angry about her lawn mower breaking down again. After you have asked a few questions, it is clear to you that she is misusing it on terrain it was never intended for. Nonetheless, she feels the problem is your fault. What do you say?

_____

_____

_____

CHAPTER 9

Becoming Immune to Intimidation

MUCH OF THIS BOOK is oriented toward working with people who are beyond their boiling point of frustration and helping them feel heard, understood, and negotiated with. But what about abusive customers who use intimidation as a finely honed weapon to get more than they deserve? For example, people who say things like, "Don't you know who I am?" or, "I'll talk to your boss if I don't get what I want."

In this chapter, we look at how to deal with toxic entitlement, wherein people cross the line from legitimate frustration to bullying and narcissism. In doing so, we explore the effective technique of non-reactivity—a combination of calmness and assertiveness—to maintain boundaries while taking away the emotional satisfaction from someone who tries to intimidate you. In addition, we touch on three important steps to achieving this: accepting a customer's self-importance, using a tool called fogging to deflect the customer's criticism, and underreacting to the customer's threats.

Ultimately, it is not the other person's words but your reactions to these words that determine the balance of power between you and an intimidator. This, in turn, governs the course and the outcome of these encounters. As with other difficult customer situations, you often have much more control over arrogant and entitled customers than you think.

Angry Customers vs. Toxic Entitlement

Take two difficult customers. Neither is happy. Both are loud, demanding, and rude. Both may be using similar threats, gestures, and foul language. Yet on the inside they are so distinct from each other that they could practically be from different species, and as a result, in order to effectively handle each of them you need to take different approaches.

What's the difference between these two individuals? One of these customers is feeling a lot like you or I might when we are unhappy. She feels wronged—and worse, she feels ignored—so she is taking out her frustrations on you. Her approach may be uncomfortable to deal with, but it ultimately springs from authentic feelings.

The other customer is following a script that has served him well for much of his life. He learned at an early age that power and intimidation give him more of what he wants. Many of us would call this person a bully; in this chapter, I use a term that perhaps better describes his psychology: *toxic entitlement*.

Most of us feel that we are entitled to whatever we deserve. With toxic entitlement, people feel they are entitled to whatever they can win. Their personal belief system does not consider other people's feelings, their agendas, or even what most people would consider to be fair and reasonable. Such customers are very different from garden-variety difficult customers. One is responding to authentic feelings; the other is gaming the system in a way that is comfortable and familiar for him.

Normal crisis communications skills do not work with these customers. They couldn't care less whether you acknowledge them or offer them face-saving alternatives; they only care that they win. And if cranking up the heat helps them win more often, so be it.

This difference holds the key for how you tell these two types of customers apart. With typical angry customers, your efforts to hear them, see their agenda, or engage in problem solving usually have some impact on their anger level. Or you can clearly tie their reactions to the gravity of the situation: Something affects them a great deal, and they are reacting to this.

With toxic entitlement, by comparison, your best efforts are met with a wall of ice. For these customers, your willingness to help is just a sign that they can keep pushing you until they get what they want. When a customer clearly doesn't care about anything but winning, regardless of the stakes, you need to adjust your communications strategy to match this situation.

Are Entitled Customers Worth Keeping?

Carol Roth, author of the bestselling book *The Entrepreneur Equation*, has a popular blog where she asks her readers to contribute their opinions on popular business issues. One month, she and I collaborated on a question specifically for this book: "How did you handle your worst customer and client situations?"

She received over fifty responses, largely from small-business owners and solo entrepreneurs, and there was a clear consensus for how best to handle difficult clients: Fire them! Here is a sample of what people had to say:

"Being in a bad relationship is not good for either party. Whether it's poor communication, a lack of respect, or not living up to expectations—you don't deserve to be treated poorly and neither do they. Talk about the issues; be accountable, fair, and ready to apologize and demand the same, but don't be afraid to break up, no matter how big the contract."—Stacy Robin, The Degania Group

"You have to know when to fire certain customers and move on. While dealing with worst-case-scenario customers, do the best you can to please them now and ensure that you don't initiate future business with them. And, giving them chocolates will also help."—Ryan Critchett, RMC TECH Mobile Repair

"We have a 'Three strikes, you're out' policy that works really well. My staff and I do a terrific job for our clients. If someone is rude, unpleasant, or just an all-around bad egg, we figure once or twice may be a coincidence, but three times is a pattern."—Jim Josselyn, Academy of Music and Drama

With the right communications techniques, it is often possible to turn around some of your most difficult customers. But when that fails, the consensus of many of the business owners surveyed here is clearly to let them go.

The Basics of Nonreactivity

Toxic entitlement springs from a fundamental difference between people. Most of us want to be reasonable and make other people happy. It bothers most of us when we cannot satisfy another person, and it really bothers us if we feel personally attacked or threatened. To entitled customers, these human traits are all weaknesses to be exploited.

This means that the core strategy we must use in dealing with toxic entitlement is what we will call nonreactivity—sending no signals to other people that their tactics are affecting us emotionally. This requires not showing any emotion. Aside from niceness being perceived as weakness, reactions indicating frustration or indignation can show we care in ways that work against us. Conversely, polite but cool detachment can form an effective barrier against toxic entitlement.

Here are three tools to use in being nonreactive:

Accept the Customer's Self-Importance

An old joke describes a wealthy businessman demanding an upgrade to first class on a sold-out flight. When he thundered, "Don't you know who I am?" the gate agent calmly got on the public address system and said, "We have a person in the terminal here who unfortunately does not know who he is. If anyone can help him, please come to the podium."

All joking aside, my recommendation is to use exactly the opposite of this approach. When you accept and acknowledge someone's importance, you neutralize it as a weapon. Compare these two exchanges:

Customer: I'm the president of a major bank, and I always insist on sitting at a window table.

You: Ma'am, we have lots of important people here, and you're going to have to wait for the first available table like everyone else at this restaurant.

Customer: I'm the president of a major bank, and I always insist on sitting at a window table.

You: You certainly are a VIP customer. Let me see what we can do for you.

How is an entitled customer going to react to these two exchanges? In the first case, you have stirred him up to defend his honor, and he is very likely to fight back or even go over your head to a manager. In the second case, he knows you get his importance, which means that even if he cannot get a window table, he cannot effectively bring up his title again. Accepting even an inflated self-image, exactly as the other person sees it, is an important tool for keeping entitled customers on topic.

Use "Fogging"

Picture yourself surrounded by a thick fog. What happens if you get angry and throw things at it? Nothing—it just sits there. Eventually you get tired of challenging the fog and move on.

This principle forms the basis of a key assertiveness skill called fogging, first described in what many consider to be the granddaddy of self-help books, Dr. Manuel J. Smith's *When I Say No, I Feel Guilty*. It involves responding to challenges by acknowledging their truth but without changing your boundaries.

Fogging is based on a truly liberating principle: You can acknowledge another person's accusations without giving in to his demands. Entitled customers will often try to convince you that you are wrong, misinformed, inexperienced, or incompetent. Fogging neutralizes these tactics without escalating the situation or getting into fruitless arguments, because you have the right to see their point while adding nothing to their argument.

This approach sounds a little like the technique of leaning into criticism described in Chapter 2; however, there's a subtle but important difference: The goal of leaning in is to mirror a customer's concerns, while the goal of fogging is to politely but effectively say, "So what?" to verbal attacks. Here are some examples:

Customer: You must be pretty new here. Everyone else lets me come in without paying the cover charge. (Note: You know better.)

You: You're right. Lots of people have been here longer than I have. Unfortunately, I still can't let you in without paying tonight.

Customer: You're really a control freak. I can't believe you won't let me exchange these items. (Note: They are nonrefundable, and you have no choice.)

You: That's true. I am pretty careful about following store policy. My apologies that I can't take these back.

Customer: You people are such incredible tightwads. I don't understand why you can't give me the Platinum package at the Bronze package price. (Note: The two packages are priced differently for a reason.)

You: Fair enough. We do try to keep a close eye on our costs. If you decide to go with us, I respect whichever package you decide to purchase.

Compare these responses with what would happen if you decided to fight back and defend yourself. First, entitled customers don't care. You will never convince them you are right anyway. Second, once you get upset, you are walking into their trap: They realize that you react to their provocations and can therefore be manipulated. Fogging short-circuits this process in a way that gets you and the customer back on track.

Underreact to Threats

What happens when entitled customers' arguments and criticisms don't work? They often start threatening you to try to get their way. They may demand to talk to your boss, or threaten to complain to other people or say bad things about you on social media.

Whatever threats they make, there is only one way to respond: Acknowledge their choices. Hand them the ax, and tell them that you respect their right to swing it if they wish. By not reacting or compromising in response to their threats, you do two important and necessary things. First, you take away their leverage over you. Second, your confidence makes them feel that much more stupid for acting the way they are. Here are some sample exchanges:

Customer: I'm going to speak to your manager about this!

You: Of course. You're most welcome to speak with her. Her name is Stacy Johnson, and she's at extension 1234.

Customer: No one's ever going to shop at your store again when I get through talking to people!

You: I'm hoping we can still find a way to make you happy, but I wouldn't dream of telling you who to talk to or not talk to.

Customer: I'm going to post about this situation on Facebook!

You: If you do, please let us know. We're always interested in honest feedback.

Remember that many more things are threatened than acted upon. For example, carrying out a threat to sue you would often require time and/or money on the part of the customer. But what if the customer backs up the bluster and carries out the threat? Respond appropriately and have faith in your chances of a fair outcome. For example, look at social media comments about other companies. When a company is disliked by consumers, negative comments can spark a feeding frenzy, but when the company is well-liked, other customers often spring to its defense. Public opinion is generally resilient enough to withstand the attacks of a single individual, especially when this person is a boor.

For all three of these techniques—accepting the customer's self-importance, fogging, and underreacting to threats—what is most notable is what is missing: any kind of self-defense or emotion. Dealing with entitled customers is like dealing with any kind of bully: They love to see you cower, compromise, and give in, which for them is like a shark seeing blood in the water. It stirs them to close in for the kill. By contrast, the only way to make them go away is to stand up to them, and the best way to do that is to communicate assertively.

Putting Nonreactivity to Work

The steps outlined here are tools in your tool kit, to be used as needed in response to whatever an entitled customer might throw at you. Let's look at an example of how each of these techniques comes into play with customers who simply want their way no matter what. Suppose a famous (but cheap) rock star who is used to getting VIP treatment without paying for it checks into the hotel you manage. Here is how the conversation might go:

Customer: Hi. The desk clerk just told me that I couldn't get a complimentary upgrade to a suite tonight. Could you fix that?

You: That's unfortunately right. I apologize for that. We're totally sold out this evening. I'll be glad to give you the nicest regular room we have available.

Customer: You don't understand. I'm headlining a major concert in town tomorrow, and I have to have a suite for me and my entourage.

You: That certainly sounds important. Did you reserve a suite with us?

Customer: I shouldn't have to. I'm a Double Priority Gold Premium member. And hotel managers are always glad to have a rock star like me staying at their hotel. It's good publicity for them.

You: It *is* an honor having you stay with us. And I really feel bad that we don't have a spare suite this evening.

Customer: Oh come on! Everyone else just bumps someone who hasn't arrived yet and gives me the suite.

You: Of course you're used to special treatment, especially when you are on tour. You're probably playing in front of several thousand people tomorrow. I hope you respect that I treat every customer here like they're special. Is there anything else we can do to make this a good night for you? Perhaps a great meal and drinks on the house?

Customer: This is totally outrageous! I'm going to talk to your boss about this!

You: You're always welcome to talk with anyone at our hotel. Here's a card with the contact information for my boss, the owner. I do apologize that we couldn't make you happy tonight.

In this case, the hotel manager correctly picked up on signals that this was an entitled rather than an unhappy customer: trumpeting his importance, expecting rather than asking for the solution he wanted, showing no concern for others, and having a dismissive reaction to anything the manager offered. In response, the manager did everything right. She acknowledged his importance, used fogging to maintain her boundaries, and underreacted to his threats.

Will the customer leave this discussion satisfied? Probably not—and that is exactly the point. Your willingness to hear this customer while holding fast to your boundaries teaches him that he cannot successfully play your emotions.

Can Entitled Customers Change?

One closing point about toxic entitlement is that no person is a stereotype. It is easy to paint entitled customers as one-dimensional bad guys and gals—and many times, they certainly act in ways that are challenging. Indeed, some of them may not be worth keeping as customers.

At the same time, there is a deeper point in learning to deal with your most arrogant and demanding customers. When you stand up to them without criticizing or reacting emotionally to them, you build respect. More important, you are creating this respect in a way that treats them with dignity and does not belittle or challenge them.

If these customers still want the product or service you are selling, you can often forge a new kind of customer relationship based on this respect. In this sense, the right communications skills can help you mine profitable relationships with people many other companies would simply give up on or cave in to. Learn to stand up to your most challenging customers, and be willing to be surprised at the impact it could have on your business.

PUTTING LEARNING INTO PRACTICE

1. You run a small wholesale business, and a new customer is offering you a large contract, but he tells you your prices are ridiculous and insists on a 40 percent discount, similar to what he says everyone else would offer him. You still would like his business. What do you say in response?

_____

_____

_____

2. You explain to a customer that she will need to pay for a repair, and she replies tartly, "I don't usually deal with people at your level anyway." What is your reply?

_____

_____

_____

3. A diner expresses dissatisfaction with his meal and wants you to cancel the bill for his entire party of eight. He is threatening to contact a local food critic if you don't. How do you respond to this?

CHAPTER 10

The Wrap-Up

ALL THINGS MUST COME TO AN END, including difficult customer transactions. And the way you end these situations is often very important. If everyone is all smiles at the end of a tough customer situation, it may not matter how hard they fought with you. By contrast, a bad ending can lead to hard feelings, further complaints, or even the whole nightmare starting all over again.

Wrapping up with difficult customers involves specific skills that leave them feeling better and prepared to move on or take the next steps. In this chapter, we focus on three techniques you can use to bring heated situations to a successful end: using a "verbal receipt" to summarize the transaction, normalizing the situation, and reaffirming the customer relationship. Together they can send you and the customer away smiling.

Understanding Good Closings

In an ideal world we would make all customers happy, and then they would shake our hands and walk away satisfied. Reality often tells another story, however. Some of your customers will have acted in ways that positively embarrass them, or leave both of you in a less-than-have-a-nice-day frame of mind.

In my view, these are perhaps the most important situations to bring to a positive close. All of us are skilled at rationalizing our own behavior, and the customer's impression of us and our business is largely formed by how the transaction ends.

Once when I was young and having one of my first out-of-town job interviews, I had a misunderstanding at a hotel. My wife asked if she could stay in our room while I was off with the interviewer. They said OK. Then when I checked out that afternoon, they charged us for a second night because she had stayed long past the checkout time. This would have been a large sum of money for us at the time, and a heated discussion ensued about who said what and when. Eventually, the hotel gave in and reversed the charge.

Was I a difficult customer that day? Probably. Was I wrong? Certainly in their minds. But in hindsight, I realize that my future business at this entire hotel chain hinged on how I was treated in that moment. Had the manager grudgingly met my demands and rudely dismissed me, I would probably have never darkened their door again. Instead, he shook my hand, told me he understood my situation, and wished me a nice day. Problem solved.

We each have a built-in advantage in trying to bring heated situations to a successful conclusion: We have all been there ourselves. Few if any of us have escaped the experience of being an angry customer. As a result, we know firsthand what a publicly humiliating experience it can be, even if we ultimately get our way. The skills discussed in this chapter will help you make things end much better for your own customers when they get angry. Let's look at how each of them works.

Give a "Verbal Receipt"

For most retail purchases, it feels strange not getting a physical receipt. This receipt serves as an acknowledgment that the transaction took place and validates what you are getting in return for your money. A "verbal receipt" can serve much the same purpose for your customers, especially when things have been challenging.

A verbal receipt is a recap of what has happened between you and the customer and what will happen from here. It is a proactive summary that goes over the steps in detail. Here are some samples of good verbal receipts:

> ▶ "Based on what we discussed, this problem should be covered as long as you have a proof of purchase from within the last

ninety days. Once you come back with a copy of your receipt, we will expedite the repair of this hard drive."

► "Our maintenance team will arrive at your house between 2 p.m. and 4 p.m. tomorrow. If there are any delays, or if you have any questions, I would like you to call our operations manager. Here is a card with her name and phone number."

► "Given everything you went through, I'm glad we could arrange at least a partial refund for this. Is there anything else we can help you with?"

A good verbal receipt does much more than just clarify your resolution to a problem. It makes you seem engaged, competent, and concerned for the customer. A more subtle point is that verbal receipts can be emotional as well as factual: They represent a good opportunity to thank customers, apologize to them, or express any other authentic feelings that help people feel better. Done well, these summaries substantially increase the odds of ending things on a good note.

Normalize the Situation

At the end of a tough transaction, one of the most powerful things you can do is make the other person feel OK about his or her behavior. Even when—listen carefully—this behavior was less than ideal. Not in a saccharine, it's-perfectly-all-right-that-you-were-a-jerk kind of way, but rather as a communion of equals: a reaffirmation that normal, healthy people get frustrated and even overinvested in customer situations.

In Chapter 7, we discussed the technique of normalizing a situation, where you validate it as being common for yourself and others. Here are some examples of using it at the end of a transaction:

► "I'm glad we were able to work this out. No one likes to go away unhappy."

► "If it were my child, I would have stood up for her interests, too."

> ► "No one wants to pay more than they have to, especially in this economy."

Some of you may wonder why you should bother to spare the feelings of difficult customers, especially after you have resolved their situation. There are several important reasons why you should at least consider this:

> ► It brings the transaction to a close quickly and peacefully.
> ► It removes the need for difficult customers to defend themselves.
> ► It makes them less likely to complain later about the situation—or about you personally.
> ► It reduces the likelihood they will come back seeking more.
> ► It may preserve their future business.

Above all, people worry that making difficult customers feel better somehow justifies their behavior and perpetuates their being difficult in the future. In reality, the opposite is usually true. Criticizing bad behavior leads people to harden their positions and defend themselves, while respect leads them to be more open to your way of thinking. By making customers feel better about what happened, you help flip their perspective in your favor and usually make them easier to deal with next time.

Reaffirm the Customer Relationship

No matter how nice you might be to a challenging customer, she probably has one remaining concern: that you have her pegged forever after as "that customer" who made your life difficult.

Why should you care about this? Because you often have a chance here to turn a crisis into a profitable opportunity. Many people who lose it in front of customer service professionals are too embarrassed to ever come back again. If you can turn around this feeling and make them feel truly welcome to come back, you have an opportunity to gain both their cooperation and their future business.

Since a customer cannot read your mind, the most powerful signal you can send that the situation is OK is to reaffirm the future of the relationship. Here are some sample statements you could use to do this:

- "If you come back next month, we plan to have some of these items on sale."
- "I'm glad we could work this out. It would be great to have you come back and try us again in the future."
- "Next time you are here, feel free to ask for me personally."

So what if your honest feelings about this customer are more like, "Please don't go away angry—just go away"? Follow your gut. If your personal radar tells you that a customer is chronically unreasonable, abusive, or threatening, there is no need to invite that person back. But most difficult situations are, at root, moments of humanity that are caused when people do not get what they want. Smooth over these situations, and you can often gain a lasting customer relationship.

Thanking Your Difficult Customers

Small-business owners sometimes wonder how to react after a client has made their lives difficult. How about thanking them?

Business consultant Karlene Sinclair-Robinson found this approach to be successful with one of her clients: "In one case, I went a step further by not just acknowledging the problem, but sending the client a handwritten 'Thank You' card for their patience, and for allowing me the opportunity to work on solving their problem." She noted that her gesture made their working relationship much easier from there: "In the end, the card concept won them over and we were able to change the outcome to their benefit, even with the changes they had to make."

Thanking people can be a powerful reaffirmation of their worth as customers. More important, it frames any difficulties you may have had in the context of a productive future relationship. And in Sinclair-

Robinson's case, the personal touch of a handwritten note got this client's attention in a very productive way.

The Right Ending: A Good Beginning

The importance of a good closing often goes far beyond the individual transaction. In a very real sense, the way you wrap things up with customers can turn into part of your brand with the public. It becomes a component of your culture and affects how others perceive you.

When I managed high-volume customer-contact operations, I put a great deal of emphasis on how we finished up with customers. In fact, I considered the way we closed a transaction to be every bit as important as the way we opened it, because final impressions often matter every bit as much as first impressions. It is a strategic tool that dovetails with your overall style with customers.

When customer situations get out of hand, good closings become even more important. Knowing how to wrap up a difficult situation does not just send customers away happier—it builds your own confidence for the future. More important, these skills can become part of a broader approach for managing the life cycle of every customer transaction.

PUTTING LEARNING INTO PRACTICE

1. A customer angrily demanded a refund for a product after going on at great length about how horrible it was. She didn't realize that you would be more than happy to give her a refund, and now she looks a little embarrassed about her behavior. What do you say?

_____

_____

_____

2. Someone calls your appliance service company and is extremely upset that no one showed up as scheduled the day before to make a repair. After rescheduling the appointment, what do you say before hanging up?

_____

_____

_____

3. A woman purchased several expensive pieces of equipment at your hardware store and was very picky and demanding about everything. You sense that she was getting exasperated with you as she kept pressing you with more questions. What might you say at the end of the transaction to help preserve her future business?

_____

_____

_____

PART III

Your Worst Customer Situations— Solved!

CHAPTER 11

You're the Boss

YOU ARE THE MANAGER of a busy public golf course in the suburbs of a major city. You just came into work, and you can tell already that it is not going to be a good morning. Why? Because a middle-aged man in golfing clothes has just burst through the front door looking enraged . . . and carrying a steering wheel in his hand.

He storms up to the counter, brushing past the people in line, and demands in a loud tone of voice to see the manager. You rush over and introduce yourself. He ignores your outstretched handshake, waving the steering wheel at you as he exclaims, "See this? Your stupid golf cart almost killed me and my family out there! My daughter has just been taken to the hospital with cuts all over!"

This is the kind of situation that customer service professionals often dread the most. It potentially has serious consequences: At least one person has been injured, and there is a real possibility of litigation. And wherever the fault of this situation ultimately lies, the customer is likely to blame you. (People don't usually tear steering wheels off of golf carts in the course of normal driving.)

What do you say in response to this person? And then how do you guide the rest of the transaction from there? In this chapter, we offer some guidelines based on the techniques discussed in the previous chapters.

Lean Into the Customer's Biggest Concerns

The customer in the previous example has just given you a critical piece of information that must jump to the top of your priority list: His daughter has been taken to the hospital, and his family was involved in an accident. Everything else is secondary at this moment. This means there is only one appropriate initial response: Lean into these concerns and proactively acknowledge them, as discussed in Chapter 2. Here is an example:

"That's terrible! How is your daughter doing? Are you injured? And how is everyone else?"

If you have ever reported an accident to the police or to your insurance company, you may recall that these transactions always start by asking how everyone is. The reason: It expresses concern for what is most important for anyone in this situation.

At this point, it is critical to give this customer whatever time and space he needs to tell his story. Use what psychologists call *minimal encourages* ("I see . . . sure . . . absolutely") to let him know that you are paying close attention to what he is telling you. Otherwise, stay out of his way until he has said whatever he feels the need to say, with as little "editing" as possible.

You might feel uncomfortable at this stage of the conversation because you have no idea how the other person is going to respond to what you say. He may calm down and reply to your questions, or he may continue to lash out at you. His words might drip with anger and sarcasm. He could even threaten you with things like legal action.

Ultimately, though, it doesn't matter what he says. Because you will do exactly the same thing in response: Lean into that response with gusto. For example:

Him: We could have all been killed out there!

You: Absolutely! Losing control of a golf cart can be really dangerous! That must have been incredibly frightening. Thank goodness no one was killed!

Him: I'll bet you were pinching pennies and skimped on maintaining these golf carts.

You: No one should ever have a mechanical failure like this happen to them.

Him: You're going to pay for this!

You: If this were my daughter, I would be reacting exactly the same way.

Note that in each of these responses, you are neither defending yourself nor contesting the other person's assertions. Your goal here is to respond to each thing this customer says in such a way that he is nodding his head to whatever you say. This means you are reflecting his reality and his emotions in a way that shows him that you get it.

Ask Good Questions

Once this person tells his story, and in all likelihood continues to vent his frustrations, you really have only one lever you can pull to try to calm him down, as discussed in Chapter 8: Ask good questions.

In the thirty seconds after you start speaking, the other person will decide whether you are with him or against him. What you say in those thirty seconds often decides whether he will ramp up or ramp down his anger. By asking questions that draw out the details of the situation, you align yourself as being on his side and start calming him down. For example:

- ► "Can you tell me what happened?"
- ► "Did you notice anything different about the golf cart before the accident happened?"
- ► "Are you and the rest of your family members able to walk around OK right now?"

By getting this person to open up about the details, you ground his anger by focusing him on the present moment. More important, you show him you are interested in the details of what happened as he sees it.

Asking the Right Questions

In a contentious situation like this, the right questions do not just serve to calm the other person down—they can also shed light on the facts of the case. For example, if this person drove your golf cart into a ditch after having a few beers, this may be a very different legal scenario than if the steering wheel simply fell off. Ask good questions, and take good notes!

Once you have established the details of the situation, your next priority should be to ask questions about his welfare and that of his family:

- ► "Is there anything I can do for you right now?"
- ► "Do you need to get in contact with anyone?"
- ► "How is the rest of your family doing right now? Is there anything they need?"

Often, showing a genuine concern for everyone's welfare represents a turning point in discussions like these. Questions like those above are not only courteous, but they serve a valuable function in the dialogue, shifting its focus from recrimination to next steps. As long as they are sincere and appropriate, these questions stand a very good chance of starting to calm the other person down.

One final note on information-gathering questions: They will only work if they are designed to hear the customer, not to challenge him. He is already in the red zone, and whether he is in the right or in the wrong, you cannot successfully explore whether he was reckless, distracted, drinking, and the like—at least not at this moment—

through direct questions. Such questions have a 100 percent probability of generating heat rather than light. Your best and perhaps only chance of getting to the real truth is to create a comfort zone that may breed more honesty.

Respond to Threats with "Can-Do" Language

When something really bad happens, many of us make a critical mistake: We try in vain to make the problem go away *right now*. In other words, we try to defend ourselves, respond equivocally, or even blame the other person, in hopes of somehow convincing him that this is not our fault. Of course, this strategy always fails miserably.

A far better approach is to accept reality and presume that the other person is going to challenge and threaten us, and then respond in a way that speaks to his interests. This is not the same as admitting fault: You probably do not have enough information at this point to do that, even if you wanted to. Rather, you focus on what you can do, as described in Chapter 6, and lead with that in each of your responses:

Him: I plan to launch an investigation of this incident!

You: Of course. We both want to find out what happened here. I am going to insist on that as well.

Him: You'll be hearing from my lawyer about this!

You: I will be happy to cooperate fully with your lawyer. I'll give you the name of our counsel.

Him: You are going to have to pay for our daughter's medical expenses!

You: We will work with you to do whatever is fair for both of us.

Note carefully that in each of these exchanges, you are not admitting liability or agreeing to compensation—yet. You simply do not know enough at this stage to make such judgments. Ultimately, the liability for this may rest with you, the golf cart manufacturer—or even the person in front of you.

At the same time, in your responses you are studiously avoiding the use of negative expectation to challenge or threaten this individual. Statements such as, "We'll have to see what our policy is" or, worse, "We need to make sure this wasn't your fault," serve no purpose at this juncture. Save them for the courtroom, if needed. Right now, your job is to choose words that de-escalate the situation, build trust, and move both of you toward the likely next steps in the process: police reports, insurance claims, legal consultations, and the like.

The Law of Reciprocity

In situations like these, there is an additional step you can take, one based on what is known as the "law of reciprocity": If you do someone an unsolicited favor, most people feel obliged to return the favor.

In the previous situation, where tempers are frayed, emotions are running high, and a daughter needs medical treatment, there is likely to be follow-up. What this customer thinks of you at the end of the transaction may have a bearing on whether he negotiates in good faith or decides to "sue the bastards" (e.g., you!). Therefore, you might consider whether an appropriate gesture might change the dynamics of the transaction.

For example, do people need rides to the hospital? Do they need a meal that you can cover as a gracious gesture? If they are from out of town, do they need lodging? You are not obligated to make gestures like these. If there is still too much tension or hostility, they may even seem patronizing or, worse, an attempt to buy them off. However, if your communications skills are working as they should, consider whether you can offer something appropriate. This could be a case where a $95 motel bill might forestall a $50,000 lawsuit.

However you handle the situation, the key is to consistently be honest and genuine, and speak to the interests of the other person. With the right words, and the right mindset, you have a very good chance of resolving situations like these in such a way that everyone wins.

CHAPTER 12

Don't You Know Who I Am?

YOU PICK UP THE PHONE WITH A POLITE, "Front desk. May I help you?" The woman's shrill voice at the other end of the line almost knocks you flat: "How dare you!"

Before you can catch your breath, she continues:

"I am a very important opera singer, and our company is here at this hotel for one night. I always make it clear when they make our reservations that I am to sleep in nothing smaller than a king bed. This room has a queen bed. How did you allow this to happen? Didn't they tell you that a diva was staying here tonight?"

"Yes, you are a diva," you think silently to yourself, as you ponder your options. The hotel is sold out. It is now past midnight. And no one ever informed the front desk that anyone staying tonight had to have a king bed. As you keep thinking, she demands to know, "What are you going to do about this outrage?"

Now it's your turn. Oh, and of course, you are the only person left on duty tonight. In this chapter, we offer some tips on how to deal with an angry customer.

Mirror the Customer's Emotions

This person is confronting you, and if you are like most people, you probably feel like defending yourself ("Ma'am, we have no record of this request") or setting limits ("You have to understand that we are sold out tonight, and there is nothing more we can do"). Both of these responses will probably just shift her from being angry to going ballistic. So what else can you do?

For starters, mirror her outrage. She is using emotionally charged phrases and terms like "How dare you" and "outrage" to try to get your attention. Matching her emotions feels like you are veering dangerously close to accepting blame, but you aren't. Instead, you are acknowledging what she is feeling and treating her complaints as being legitimate *to her*. And frankly, it is your only hope of getting her to calm down and talk rationally with you. Try lines like these:

▶ "That's outrageous! I don't blame you at all for wanting your usual bed."

▶ "What a rude surprise, especially the night before a performance!"

▶ "I can tell by your tone of voice how much you were inconvenienced tonight."

How will she respond to this? Perhaps she will calm down. Perhaps she will continue ranting. Either way, one thing is clear: If you don't acknowledge how upsetting this is to her, it is practically guaranteed that she will get even more upset. Next, you must move on to problem solving.

Explore the Options

You are basically a very nice person. In a situation like this, you would probably love nothing better than to move this guest to a room with a king bed posthaste. Unfortunately, you do not have that option, unless you want to go wake up and move another guest—which Ms. Diva would probably love you to do. So at this point you have two choices: (1) ask her what she might like in lieu of a king bed, or (2) go for the LPFSA (Low Probability Face-Saving Alternative) problem-solving technique we discussed in Chapter 8.

This guest is so angry that it may feel hard to ask what she wants—for fear she will demand a king's ransom, or your head on a platter—but you must move forward and trust in your communications skills to handle whatever she responds with. Otherwise you will be blindly proposing solutions without ever making her part of the process, which is usually a recipe for disaster. Try framing your question something like this:

> "First, I want to apologize that you weren't put in a room with a king bed, and I intend to find out why this didn't happen. If I could move you right now, I would gladly do that. Unfortunately, we are completely sold out tonight, and I don't have another room available. I realize you wanted a larger bed, but I wanted to explore if there is anything else we can do for you to make this a good stay tonight. Perhaps something nice from room service?"

This statement apologizes for the situation, even though the fault of the situation is not yet clear (and is irrelevant at this stage). It also promises action, summarizes the situation, and engages her to solve it with you. How will she respond?

- ► She may propose a mutually acceptable solution, such as breakfast in bed tomorrow. If so, congratulations: You're done.
- ► She may continue railing on about how unacceptable this is. Keep acknowledging this and offering solutions.
- ► She may propose something unacceptable, like a free week's stay in the future. In this case, acknowledge her ("I can't blame you for being upset enough to want that") and calmly keep responding with what you *can* do.

In each of these cases, you are now engaged in a totally mechanical process of acknowledgment and problem solving, as outlined in Chapter 6. Keep working the process, and see if a solution presents itself.

Use the LPFSA

If you are still stuck at this point, the LPFSA may represent your best chance of closing the transaction on a peaceful note. Examples of such alternatives might include offering to try to arrange a room at a nearby hotel (she is not likely to want to leave at midnight, especially with her entourage), or offering to swap rooms if other guests vacate theirs prior to her bedtime.

Using the LPFSA effectively requires disclosing that your suggestions are low-probability alternatives. Moreover, the customer needs to perceive that you are sincerely trying to be helpful and not just trying to get rid of her. That said, creatively brainstorming options can send a powerful signal to the guest that you are engaged with her problem and thinking on her behalf.

Show a Personal Interest

Most desk clerks would focus on this guest's problems, and her anger, in situations like this one. A few people, however, would take things a step further and show a personal interest in her by using appropriate questions and/or compliments. For example, some might ask her about her performance, explore how sleep affects her singing, or express interest in the fact that she is an opera star.

You do have to be careful here: The wrong kinds of questions can sound patronizing, especially if you haven't done enough yet to try to resolve her concerns. Follow your gut on how to proceed. Many bad customer relationships can be turned around when you honor the customer's self-importance, as discussed in Chapter 9. When you respect your guests as people, with their own unique gifts and needs, even angry and arrogant ones can ultimately leave with a good impression of you and your service.

CHAPTER 13

The Concert That Never Was

LAST NIGHT'S EVENT was billed as the biggest rock concert of the century, and Julia and her best friend couldn't wait to attend. First, the headliners had been Julia's favorite band since childhood, and she had never seen them live. Second, she won her tickets in a major, corporate-sponsored giveaway. Third, she traveled over two hundred miles to a major city to see this concert. It was going to be a very special night.

Except that it never happened. The concert promoter had printed special tickets just for this corporate giveaway in the sponsor's color and logo, but unfortunately, the event facility was never told about them. So when Julia and her friend arrived for the concert, they were turned away. No amount of pleading, coaxing, or tears could persuade any of the event staff to let them in. In fact, when she finally got to speak to a manager, he threatened to have them both arrested for forging their tickets.

The next day, Julia appeared on a major morning television program describing how she and her friend were treated, and her story became part of the national news feed. You are a public relations representative for the corporation that awarded her the tickets, and have been asked by your management to contact Julia and "clean up the mess." How would you handle this? In this chapter, we examine how to effectively handle a very public incident that your organization ultimately caused.

Talk with the Customer First

First and foremost, you need to reach out to Julia; she deserves the respect of being contacted before you respond in public. Her reactions, and her expectations, will also help frame your public response to this situation.

So how is Julia likely to react? She will probably be pretty angry; after all, she was upset enough to take her story to the media. She also was wronged at a very fundamental level: She was hoping to attend a concert by her favorite band and instead ended up being turned away and threatened with arrest. Finally, the problem was completely your fault.

This may not be an easy conversation to have, but it can follow a very clear process similar to the one outlined in Chapters 2 and 3: Lean into her criticism and acknowledge her as deeply as possible by using validation and identification. You can also help defuse her anger by asking good assessment questions, as discussed in Chapter 8. Here is a sample:

Julia: I was dreaming about this concert for weeks, and it turned into a complete nightmare!

You: *(leaning in)* This sounds horrible, Julia. *(validation)* I know everyone was really looking forward to this concert. This couldn't have turned out worse for you, and I feel terrible that we were responsible for it.

Julia: The people at the auditorium made my friend and I feel like common criminals! You have absolutely no idea how humiliated I was.

You: *(identification)* I can't even begin to imagine what that must have been like for you! That sounds really awful. Especially when you did absolutely nothing wrong. *(assessment)* Tell me more about what happened.

The key ingredients to this dialogue are to acknowledge everything she says, respect the legitimacy of each of her feelings, and learn as much as you can about the situation, while making no effort whatsoever at this stage to defend yourself. How long should you continue this process? Until Julia has had her say. Give her the time and space to express whatever feelings she needs to, and respond to each and every one of them.

Finally, you need to have a clear apology early in the conversation that takes full ownership of what happened, acknowledges its consequences for her, and promises to make things right. Here is an example:

> "Julia, we caused a heartbreaking situation for you this week. Because of our mistakes, you not only had to miss the concert after traveling so far, but the situation was handled in a way that was infuriating and humiliating for you. I want to apologize on behalf of everyone who was involved, and let you know that we will do everything in our power to make this up to you."

Practice Creative Service Recovery

What happens next, after you have done enough acknowledgment and apologized for the situation? Usually the conversation will naturally turn to what needs to happen from here. We call this phase service recovery because it involves recovering from a service failure. Once the topic comes up, invite her to be as frank as possible:

Julia: You people need to pay for what happened to me.

You: If this had happened to me, I would certainly want restitution too. Please tell me what would make this situation right for you.

Then listen to and validate each and every thing she asks for, even if it is outrageous. Your goal at this stage is not to rule on what you will do for her; it is for her to feel completely heard. For example, one good way to respond to unrealistic requests is the paraphrasing technique described in Chapter 3:

Julia: I want to go on tour with this band for the next year!

You: So you would enjoy hanging out and traveling with the band. That sounds like it would be a lot of fun!

Does this response sound strange, especially knowing that your company would not be in a position to comply with this request, and that the band itself would be unwilling to agree? Actually, it is one of the very best things you can say, because it both hears her and uses the language of an ally—and people ultimately tend to negotiate better with someone who is being a friend.

Ultimately, you will leave this conversation with an idea of how Julia and her friend are feeling and what will be needed to make them happy. In Chapter 6, we discussed how to frame problem solving in terms of what you can do for the customer's interests. In addition to compensating her for her tickets and her travel expenses, consider things like:

- ► Flying Julia and her friend to another stop on the concert tour
- ► Giving her front row seats
- ► Arranging for her to meet the band or get autographs
- ► Inviting her to bring more of her friends or family members
- ► Giving her valuable collectibles or souvenirs from the concert

When you are trying to right a very public wrong like this, you should be prepared to overcompensate for what happened—not only to make Julia and her friend feel better about what happened, but because you are perceived by the public as a wealthy corporation that wronged an innocent girl. And because the alternative may well be an expensive and publicly damaging lawsuit. Ideally, the best solution should make everyone involved feel like they came away a winner.

Super Bowl XLV: First Impressions Matter

In February 2011, as the NFL prepared to host Super Bowl XLV in Arlington, Texas, over twelve hundred fans learned at the last minute that the temporary seating sections for which they had tickets had not been completed in time. While many of these fans were seated elsewhere, four hundred were greeted with a terse form letter telling them they had no seats and would receive refunds of three times the face value of their tickets. Many of them ended up watching the game on television monitors inside a field-level hospitality area or on standing-room-only platforms.

Many of these fans reacted with outrage, particularly those who had spent thousands of dollars on airfare and hotels to travel with their families to the game. The NFL soon sweetened its offer to include a ticket to the next year's Super Bowl, and then later the options of a trip to a future Super Bowl with airfare and hotel expenses, $5,000 cash, or reimbursement of more than $5,000 with documented expenses. This was not enough to placate all of the fans, and a class-action lawsuit against the NFL continues to work its way through the courts.

Respond to the Public

You have another set of "customers" to placate besides Julia and her friend: the public at large. Because this situation has played out in the media, you will need to make a public apology, and this response may become an important part of your company's brand image.

To the untrained observer, corporate public relations can sometimes seem like a fun-house mirror that distorts reality: Problems become "issues," an outrage is framed as an "inconvenience," and a big mistake can turn into a "misunderstanding." Even worse, PR statements are frequently wrapped in a thick layer of prose about how great the company is, even when it did not act great at all. They are often rife with the kinds of triggering catchphrases we recommended avoiding in Chapter 4.

Here you must take off your PR hat and become real, authentic, and contrite. Like the apology suggested for Julia, your public response must express regret, take full ownership of the situation, and document your response to it. If this response connects with people at a personal level, it will go a long way to limit the damage to your reputation.

CHAPTER 14

I'll Be Suing You

"SUE IS ON LINE 1 FOR YOU," your assistant says dryly, and you pick up the phone.

"Hello, Sue! How can I help you?" you say with a smile. "My name is Alice," the other person responds tersely. "And I am calling to let you know that I am planning to sue you."

Before you can say a word in response, she continues: "We purchased a pallet-load of your chairs for the conference room at our clinic, for people attending our educational programs. Since we are a weight-loss facility, many of our clients are morbidly obese. But we had no idea that so many of them would collapse under people when they sat on them."

"That's horrible!" you exclaim, and she cuts you off before you can say anything else. "Someone brought a video camera to one of our meetings and caught one of your chairs collapsing under a new client. The video has gone viral on YouTube, and people are ridiculing our business all over the Internet. Now the client is demanding that we cover her medical expenses. This whole incident is ruining our business, and it's all your fault!"

Now it is finally your turn to speak. What do you say from here? In this chapter, we look at how you can communicate in a way that gives you your very best chance to stay out of the courtroom.

Do Not—Repeat, Do Not—Defend Yourself First

The first thing to consider here is what *not* to say in response to this caller. Most people's strongest instinct would lead them to commit a fatal flaw: defending themselves. As we discussed in Chapter 8, self-defense generally only makes angry customers angrier.

Suppose, for example, that you respond with something that is absolutely true in defense of your product. What would be wrong with a statement like this:

"Ma'am, our chairs do have a published weight limit of 280 pounds."

Here is what would be wrong: It would have exactly the opposite effect that you intend. Let's translate this statement into what customers hear: "I couldn't care less that someone was injured on one of our chairs, or that your reputation is suffering as a result. We plan to hide behind every technicality we can, and you will probably have to sue us before you ever get our attention." If you accomplish anything here, it would probably be to motivate the person to find a lawyer who will propose a hefty financial settlement for the customer's future loss of business.

This is not to say that you should never defend yourself, just that that should come later in the process, as you negotiate a settlement (or, in the worst case, face off in court). In the meantime, trying to "educate" a customer that she shouldn't sue is a fool's errand. Instead, focus on hearing her complaint and positioning yourself as an ally: Empathize with her, ask good questions, and acknowledge her view of what happened, which is not the same as accepting blame.

The thought of a lawsuit is scary for most of us. The mere mention of the word brings up mental images of being in court, spending large amounts of money, and dealing with lawyers. Remember, though, that when someone is threatening to sue you but has not done so yet, it is a sign that she has a strong grievance and is giving you a chance to resolve it. This means that the right language can keep you both in dialogue and help move both of you toward a solution.

Explore Solutions

Another painless thing you can do at this stage without admitting liability is to explore what might resolve the situation, as outlined in
Chapter 8. There may also be gestures you can offer, without admitting fault, that could build trust and goodwill with the customer. For
example:

You: I agree, this is a terrible situation. What do you think we could
   do from here to help you?

Alice (sarcastically): Short of asking Mr. Internet to stop streaming
   this viral video of our client collapsing on your chair, I'm not really
   sure.

You: Actually, I am thinking along those lines. We would be happy to
   approach the key people who are posting this video and negotiate
   if they would be willing to take it down. Would it be OK with you
   if we gave that a try?

The client may ultimately make a proposal: perhaps compensation
for the client's medical injuries, or replacement chairs that are
stronger. This becomes a starting point for negotiation, which in all
likelihood will extend beyond the bounds of this phone call. Legal
advice may be appropriate at this stage, since offering a settlement
involves the possibility of admitting liability or setting precedents, but
your ultimate goal is to create a win-win solution for both parties.

Frame the Benefits

In Chapter 7, we discussed framing solutions in ways that sound palatable to the customer. Once you have a resolution you would be comfortable offering, you have two objectives in framing it: (1) entice the
customer to want your solution, and (2) make it much more attractive
than the prospect of suing you—a path that might yield a greater
reward for the customer, but at the risk of paying lawyers, spending
time in court, and possibly losing the case. Here is an example of what
you might say:

"We realize that you've been through a very awkward and public situation that involved our chairs. Even though we have a published weight limit for these chairs, our bigger concern is making things right for everyone involved. We're prepared to offer you a generous discount on a more sturdy model of replacement chair, and would also be happy to help address the negative social media publicity that has happened recently. We respect your decision, but we're hoping this offer will help resolve things in a way that's easier for everyone."

This statement achieves several important objectives. It acknowledges what has happened to the customer, describes your defense in a factual and neutral way, and sells the benefits of the solution versus entering into litigation. Notice also a subtle but important phrase: "We respect your decision." This reaffirms the customer's control over her decision. Ironically, she will probably be more likely to accept your resolution if she feels it is not being dictated to her in a take-it-or-leave-it fashion.

Can Apologies Prevent Lawsuits?

Hospitals are often loathe to disclose medical errors for fear of stirring up lawsuits. But what happens when they start proactively taking ownership of these mistakes?

A study published in 2010 examined what happened when the University of Michigan Health System (UMHS) implemented a new model for handling medical errors, involving full disclosure of what happened, a formal apology, and an offer of compensation. The results? New claims fell by 36 percent, lawsuits decreased by over 50 percent, and costs decreased by close to 60 percent.

UMHS is unusual in having its own staff and a single insurer, and therefore being the only party responding to a patient's medical errors; further research is needed to see if these findings generalize to other health systems. But at least in this one case, honesty may be the most cost-effective policy.

CHAPTER 15

Quelling a Social Media Firestorm

YOUR COOKIE COMPANY has always been ahead of the times, particularly when it comes to using social media with customers. You have a fan page on Facebook, a Twitter account, and a thriving online community where people post questions and answers about your products. If you were any more connected with your customers, you would probably have to move in with them.

One day, a customer posted a negative comment on your Facebook page, complaining that his last order from you arrived late. Worse, because his settings are set to only show your posts rather than to view everyone's, he mistakenly thought you were deleting his comments. Outraged, he began mass-posting hateful comments about you online. Now what do you do?

The rule in customer service used to be that if someone was happy, he would tell four people, and if they were unhappy, he would tell eleven people. Today, thanks to the rise of social media, those numbers are way off. When musician Dave Carroll watched baggage handlers toss around and break his expensive guitar on a United Airlines flight, and then got nowhere trying to get the airline to compensate him, he composed a song, "United Breaks Guitars," that has now had over twelve million views on YouTube. The airline finally offered to make things right after a firestorm of negative publicity, and today United actually uses this video in its customer service training.

When a customer gets mad at you and starts acting out on social media, you have two agendas. The first is to take care of the problem. The second is to let the public know you are taking care of the problem—and better yet, for the customer to help with this. In this chapter, we offer some guidelines for how you might handle this situation.

Be Real

In Chapter 4, we discussed avoiding trigger phrases that infuriate customers. In a world of social media, this includes most of the stilted, corporate prose that most companies use in their written or email communications, such as, "Sir, we are investigating your request," or, "We regret to inform you . . ." When used online, phrases like these sound like they were uttered by a robot.

Instead, use genuine, accessible language—the kind you might use with a good friend over lunch. As part of a technology that started with young people, social media have brought with them a greater expectation of informality. So, as we have recommended throughout the book, lead by acknowledging the customer. In this case, you might start your message with something like, "This sounded like a pretty frustrating experience. We want to make this situation right."

Be Quick

What you say is very important, but how soon you say it is almost as important. Customer complaints can go viral quickly through social media. Moreover, people look at your response time as a measure of how much you care about your customers. This means that comments in cyberspace can't wait for your next weekly committee meeting. It is important to provide a same-day reply, even if it is just to tell someone you are looking into the problem.

Make your reply to customer criticism all about the customer. Social media are magnifying glasses for how responsive you are to customers. Even if you are technically correct, focusing on defending or explaining yourself can be like throwing fresh bait into shark-infested waters: It can cause a feeding frenzy of negative responses.

Instead, validate legitimate criticisms and keep a laser focus on doing what is right for the customer.

For example, suppose this customer's shipment was delayed because he chose a cheaper ground-shipping option with no guaranteed delivery date. In this case, you might say, "Even though we don't have control over ground shipping once our cookies leave the factory, two weeks is a long time to wait. Especially for cookies!" Or suppose the problem was your fault because his order was lost. In this instance, you should lean in and completely own his complaint the way we discussed in Chapter 2: "We messed up, pure and simple. Your order got lost in our system. That was inexcusable." Then, in either case, propose a fair solution to the issue, or, better yet, get in touch personally, as we describe in the next step.

Reach Out to the Person Behind the Keyboard

When you communicate with people in cyberspace, you still aren't quite a real person to them. They haven't connected you with a name and a face. Often, social media complaints are best used as an entree to contact someone in person and resolve the issue.

In this particular case, personal contact is essential. Since the customer is unaware that you are not responding due to a technical problem on his end, the only way to straighten things out is to get in touch. Your goal is not to point out his mistake, but rather to normalize it as something that could happen to anyone, as discussed in Chapter 10. Then you can negotiate whatever would be needed (and appropriate) to make him happy.

Trust the Will of the Crowd

Today, companies often fear that someone will post something negative about them using social media. But check out other companies' social media sites and you will discover that the general mood of customers is reflected pretty accurately. In cases where a company truly has poor service in the public eye, complaints can often spark a feeding frenzy where other people chime in and express their displeasure. But if your company has a strong service reputation, something amazing often happens: People respond to complaints by jumping to your defense.

This means that although you should work hard to address concerns that people post online, there is no need to overreact to an individual negative post. In much the same way that people's reputations are formed in the real world, your organization's reputation within social media is truly an aggregate of everyone's overall impressions.

The example in this chapter was paraphrased from a true story, and here is how it actually ended: When the customer realized that the company had not deleted any of his comments, he felt silly, took them down, and publicly announced that the company had taken care of the situation. Being proactive and focusing on the customer's interests—even when complaints are unfair or misguided—will generally have a strong ripple effect on how people talk publicly about your organization online.

CHAPTER 16

Just Plane Terrible

YOU ARE A GATE AGENT for Good Time Airlines. But tonight, you are not having a good time. Why? Because of the long line of angry-looking people who have been queuing up in front of your podium.

You see, telling one or two people that they aren't going to get where they want to go is no fun. Telling the two hundred people who just disembarked from the Boeing 767 at your gate is even less fun. And worst of all, these people have been on and off this plane for hours during this winter storm—taxiing out, waiting for the plane to be deiced, waiting too long to take off, and coming back to the gate again. Now weather conditions have finally shut down the airport for the evening.

Your job is to tell these two hundred people:

➤ They are stuck here for the night.

➤ Your airline does not pay hotel expenses for weather-related cancellations like this one.

➤ The nearest hotel with rooms available is the Dingy Acres Motel, a half hour's drive from the airport. And yes, it is as bad as it sounds.

➤ You will book them on the first available departure tomorrow. With emphasis on *available*.

You can expect there to be a number of very unhappy people. Many of them will be upset with you and your airline. Some may desperately need to get somewhere for a specific occasion. More than a few will feel it is totally unacceptable to spend the night at the airport. You have just signed on to the computer at your podium and are about to speak with the first passenger in line. Aside from wishing you the very best of luck, in this chapter, we offer some techniques to help get you through a situation that's beyond your control.

Be Present

First, understand the depth of frustration that many of these people are feeling. Some may be seasoned travelers who have been through this many times before, but others will still be trying to wrap their head around the situation. They were on the plane and so close to being at their destination that they could taste it. Perhaps they are afraid to fly and now have to face their fears all over again. Or perhaps there are consequences for them, such as missing a wedding, a funeral, or a paid performance.

The first and most important part of handling each passenger is to respond empathetically by paraphrasing and acknowledging whatever that person leads with. For example:

Passenger: I am missing an important business meeting tomorrow!

You: That's terrible! It seems unfair to have a snowstorm shut down air traffic right when you have important business to take care of.

Passenger: I've been dreading this flight for weeks, and now I have to go through it all over again!

You: That must be miserable! You were probably hoping this would all be over with tonight. What can we do to help you be comfortable in the meantime?

This is a very important step, and also a completely mechanical one: Take whatever the passenger leads with and hand those words, thoughts, and feelings back with empathy, as we have emphasized throughout this book. Connecting with these customers as people will usually make everything that follows go much easier.

Deliver the Bad News in Stages

You are about to tell many of these passengers a number of things they do not want to hear: that they are stuck at the airport for the evening, that lodging options are not the best, and that they will have to wait for the first available flight the next day. How you word this news will often make all the difference in how they react to it.

Chapter 5 describes a process for how to stage bad news in a way that makes it easier for people to accept it: a good introduction, a proactive summary of the options, and an empathetic response. Here is an example of putting that into practice in this situation:

Passenger: Darn, they canceled this flight! Can you get me out of here tonight? Or you'll put me up somewhere, correct? (Note: The answer is "no" to both of these questions.)

You: *(introduction)* Let me walk you through what options we have here. *(proactive summary)* I can confirm a seat for you on the next flight available to your destination right now. This flight leaves nine hours from now, which takes us into tomorrow morning. As for lodging, we do provide lodging for mechanical delays or actions of the airline. Unfortunately, we can't offer this in the case of a weather-related cancellation such as tonight's. Do you think you might prefer to relax here at the airport, or could I help you arrange a hotel room at your expense?

Because you have laid out the options in a way that is factual, empathetic, and doesn't lecture the passenger or say "no," you have a much better chance of getting a constructive response. But suppose he still is not happy about what he is hearing and lets you know about it? Let's continue:

Passenger: That stinks! I'm really exhausted.

You: *(empathetic response)* You must be exhausted. I certainly wouldn't like being stuck on a plane for as long as you were. *(proactive sum-*

mary) I'm pretty familiar with this airport. Would you like to know some places where you might relax for a few hours?

Passenger: I'd really rather be at a hotel, even if I have to pay for it myself.

You: *(empathetic response)* I can't blame you at all. *(proactive summary)* Here is what you will be looking at. Because we are located far from town, the nearest lodging is at the Dingy Acres Motel. I do want you to know that it is a half hour drive from here, and it is a very modest facility. But there are rooms available tonight, and I could give you a discount coupon for it if you wish.

Passenger: Yecch! That sounds miserable. How about a major chain hotel?

You: *(empathetic response)* Very good question. Most major chains are located in town, approximately an hour from the airport by public transportation. Would you like to look at some of those?

Passenger: No, that is a long way away. I'll probably stick it out at the airport tonight. Look, I appreciate all of your help.

You: *(empathetic response)* My pleasure, Mr. Jones. Let us know if there is anything else we can do to help, and hopefully we'll have you on your way again in a few short hours.

Compare these responses to the snippy, "I'm sorry, sir, we can't do that" ones that are all too common in stressful customer situations, as we discussed in Chapter 4. This is where the right words can make a big difference. As long as you keep working the mechanics of responding empathetically and offering options, most customers will eventually calm down and cooperate with you, even when the news is not good.

Reframe the Situation

In the example above, you may have noticed that the agent used the reframing technique outlined in Chapter 7 to make the situation seem more palatable to the passenger. Notice how these specific phrases were thoughtfully chosen to defuse the situation:

- ▶ "Relax here at the airport" (rather than *stuck at the airport*).

- ▶ "Very modest facility" (rather than *dumpy motel*)

- ▶ "On your way again in a few short hours" (rather than *stranded overnight*)

- ▶ "Some places where you might relax for a few hours" (rather than *hope you like sleeping in a chair*)

This agent is also framing the problem-solving process in terms of what is possible rather than what isn't possible, as discussed in Chapter 6. Instead of saying, "You will have to wait until tomorrow," he is saying, "I can confirm a seat for you on the next flight available." These subtle but important linguistics employ the language of an ally and let the customer know that he is focused on helping.

Note also that the one thing we are not reframing is the customer's experiences. If he is complaining about being exhausted, then by golly, he is exhausted. And if something is bothering him, then it legitimately bothers him. When you maximize customers' concerns while framing positive solutions for them, you can often guide them skillfully into calming down and accepting the situation.

Don't Take It Personally

In an ideal world, passengers would understand that you do not control the weather. Unfortunately, in a less-than-ideal situation such as this, they are at great risk of taking out their frustrations on you. Dr. David Burns, a psychiatrist, refers to this as "emotional reasoning": You feel lousy, and you (incorrectly) blame others for making you feel that way.

This means that some passengers may invent some blame and hurl it back at you: You should have known about this weather and planned ahead. You should have gotten them off the plane sooner. Your policies are horrible and unfair. Your response? Do not lead with trying to correct them, but rather be present with their frustrations:

Passenger: If you could have gotten us back to the terminal sooner, we could have gotten on another flight!

You: Tonight has frustrated the heck out of a lot of our customers. I don't blame you for being upset. What can we do to help you from here?

If it makes people feel better, you may choose to eventually explain the reality of the situation, whether it is to correct a misperception or to take ownership of a legitimate grievance. Just understand that it is more important to first acknowledge and validate what people are feeling. Once people feel that you get them, it becomes much easier to engage in productive dialogue.

This scenario is based on my own experience being stranded overnight at a major airport in a winter storm, on my way back from a speaking engagement in the Midwest. As a frequent traveler, I personally handled the situation with kindness and good humor (in fact, I greeted the gate agent with a smile and the statement, "No stress in your life tonight!"), but many people were agitated and upset. One person, for example, forced his way to the front of the line while railing loudly against the airline, and others grumbled about the amount of time they had been cramped on the jet or how the situation impacted their plans.

While I was in line, I noticed an interesting dynamic in how the gate agents handled this situation. All tried their best to be polite, but some would visibly shut down once a customer started getting angry, avoiding eye contact and saying as little as possible. Others were able to engage these customers, and those agents had much more success in defusing their anger. Even in situations with many angry people, the right words, thoughtfully chosen, give you your very best chance to keep things under control.

CHAPTER 17

Anger Management

YOU ARE THE NEW PERSON at a busy private gym and weight-training facility. It is your first week on the job, and you and your coworker Frank are sitting around talking about some of the regular customers you will be dealing with. Before long, he brings up Bruno, a muscle-bound daily customer who intimidates everyone and "is always angry about something." You smile and respond, "Like a barking dog?" "More like an ogre," your partner replies with a laugh. "Big, intimidating, and turns several shades of green as you talk to him."

About an hour later, with a line of customers at your counter, in walks Bruno—and sure enough, Frank was right. He isn't very happy. In fact, his face is turning red as he raises his voice and pokes his finger on the counter for emphasis. "Look at these machines! The weights haven't been put back in the rack, and half of them haven't been wiped down by the last person. I *demand* that you drop everything *right now* and clean up the weight room."

"Hey, my shift is over, so I'll let you take Bruno this time," Frank says, in a stage whisper, as he slips out the back of the room. Three people are in line ahead of Bruno. In this chapter, we focus on how to respond to someone with an anger-management problem.

Frame the Situation

Before you even open your mouth to respond to Bruno, let's check in on your own feelings here. Do you feel frightened? Intimidated? Uncomfortable?

In this case, these very normal human emotions are all based on a mirage. Bruno is a big, muscular man with a booming voice. How do we process these physical cues? As though we were at risk of being physically assaulted. And Bruno, who is used to getting his way through intimidation, would love for you to keep perceiving the situation that way.

In reality, he is not going to hit you—unless, of course, he has a thing for jail cells, lawsuits, and getting permanently banned from his favorite gym. So first and foremost, remember that all you are dealing with here are words. Loud, angry words to be sure, but words nonetheless. He is no more of an actual threat to you than a little kid with a squeaky, high-pitched voice.

One of the other things you may be feeling is anger at Bruno, especially since he regularly uses intimidation as a way to get what he wants. You may be tempted to respond to him in a way that is designed to "put him in his place." Of course, you have the right to set appropriate boundaries with him, but a stance of pushing back on him at first is likely to be doomed to failure.

So before you say anything to Bruno, frame the situation correctly. Tell yourself that you are perfectly safe, that he can express any feelings that he wishes to, and that whatever happens, you will respond to him professionally. Now, let's look at how to do this.

Acknowledge Bruno

There is only one response that will give you any hope of getting Bruno to calm down: Acknowledge everything he says. Wherever possible, use the techniques of validation and identification discussed in Chapter 3 to respond to each of his outbursts. And do it with as much gusto as possible. For instance:

Bruno: Look at these machines! The weights haven't been put back in the rack, and half of them haven't been wiped down by the last person.

You: That's *terrible*! People should know better than to leave a mess for others at this gym. That bothers me too.

This first response is where human nature trips most of us up. Since Bruno is demanding our immediate attention and putting us on the defensive, our first instinct is to defend ourselves, or to set boundaries with him. Too often, we are tempted to respond with statements like these:

- ▶ "There are people in line ahead of you. Please wait your turn."
- ▶ "Only a couple of the weights are out of the rack. Could you just put them back?"
- ▶ "I'm sorry, we can't possibly keep an eye on everyone who uses the equipment."

News flash: Bruno doesn't care about the people in line. He doesn't care how many weights are off the rack. He certainly does not approve of your lack of oversight. And his explosive temper may well come, in part, from learning that anger moves people off excuses and boundaries like these and gets him what he wants. So statements that sound even the least bit like these simply cause you to walk right into his trap.

Your only possible hope of calming him down is to meet him where he is. Here are some other examples:

Bruno: This is wasting my valuable workout time!

You: Absolutely. No one likes to pick up after some slob who came before you.

Bruno: You don't keep this gym in adequate shape. You're falling down on the job.

You: I wouldn't be happy if I was seeing this stuff happen regularly either, so I'm glad you're letting us know.

Remember that acknowledging people is never the same as giving in to them. Use language that shows Bruno you understand him, and you have your best hope of getting him to back off and listen to you.

Frame Your Response

Here is the key moment of the discussion: Bruno is insisting that you drop everything, ignore the people in line ahead of him, and take care of him first. Do you give in to his demands?

No, you do not. That would not be fair to your other customers. More important, it would be enabling his penchant for bullying people. But the way you set your boundaries will mean everything to the success of this situation.

Let's be honest. Most of us would normally respond to Bruno by trying to "correct" his behavior and focusing on our boundaries with language like this:

Bruno: I *demand* that you drop everything *right now* and clean up the weight room.

You: You'll have to wait until I'm done with the people in line ahead of you.

It is your perfect right to say this. It is technically the correct answer. And it is the policy that is most fair to everyone. So now, how likely is Bruno to respond by saying, "Golly, you are right. I will wait my turn."? Not very. You must try another approach if you want to avoid a confrontation.

In Chapter 6, we discussed how to frame your response around the customer's agenda, not your own. This is the key for how you respond to Bruno's demands. Try this:

Bruno: I *demand* that you drop everything *right now* and clean up the weight room.

You: Of course. I'm going to hurry as much as I can with everyone here so you can get back to your workout.

How will he respond to this? Hopefully more calmly, because you have played his agenda back to him and honored it, while keeping your boundaries. But a more subtle point here is that it doesn't really matter how he responds. All that matters is what *you* say—and whatever his provocations might be, you can keep responding with the simple, mechanical technique of framing your response around his agenda:

Bruno: My time is more important than these people. I'm a paying customer.

You: Your time *is* very important. I don't like anything holding up my workouts either. Give me just a little time, and I'll jump right on this.

Bruno is probably demanding two things here: getting what he is asking for, and respect for his concerns. By framing your response around these concerns, you give him something tangible in return for his complaint: the promise of a resolution. In the process, you also honor his second goal of being respected for how he feels.

Execute the Endgame

The language proposed here will probably give you your very best chance of making things go more constructively with Bruno. But he does have a pretty short fuse. What if what you say doesn't work, and he keeps ranting?

Calmly repeat yourself. In Chapter 6 we discussed the power of repetition in convincing people that their anger won't benefit them. Be prepared to go two or three rounds with Bruno, and after a while he should start to realize that he is only making himself look bad, rather than getting what he wants. And after the third time, extinguish the effect of his anger further by focusing on your other customers—perhaps politely holding up your index finger to remind him that his turn is over, and you are now focused on someone else.

At the end of the day, Bruno is only going to persist in behaviors that benefit him. He may be angry, but he probably isn't stupid. And if you calmly stick to your communications process and execute it, even if he still is not happy, he will most likely decide his best interests are served by calming down and waiting.

What is the worst that can happen in this situation? Again, he is highly unlikely to act out violently. Of course, there are customers whose behavior crosses the line, and times when you need to go for your worst-case solutions: asking people to leave, calling for security, and so forth. But perhaps the key point here is that when you use the right language, the need for interventions like these is much less common than you might imagine. The odds are very good here that Bruno will eventually calm down, wait for you to finish, and then go back to his workout.

In Chapter 8, we looked at a more detailed approach for handling angry customers involving the use of the highest acknowledgment level possible, asking good questions, and then shifting the discussion to problem solving. A process like this would be appropriate once Bruno reaches the *front* of the line. In the meantime, the steps outlined here serve as a good approach for managing the situation until it is his turn to speak with you.

Relationship Building

One closing note. Remember how your coworker Frank described Bruno as a regular customer whose anger was well known? This raises what may be a deeper issue with your most difficult regular customers: How do they feel about you?

We all react differently to friends than to foes. If Bruno comes in, says little, works out, and leaves, you and your coworkers may seem like faceless robots he feels he can react to. But if you show an interest in Bruno—get to know him as a person, ask how he is doing, and champion his aspirations—you may start becoming real and human to him. This, in turn, is often the key to turning Bruno into a nicer person who is much easier to deal with.

CHAPTER 18

Not So Smart

AN ELDERLY MAN walks into your electronics store and slams a box down on the counter. "This is the third time I've had to bring back one of your stupid, defective computers," he says, loudly and angrily. "None of them have worked!"

You ask him politely what went wrong, and he exclaims that he can't even select anything on the screen with the mouse. Noting that this was the third computer he has had to return, you offer to set it up in the store and test it for him. As you do so, he also shares that he is a retired professor who is "pretty smart" at most things.

After you plug in and power up the computer, he grabs the mouse, holds it in mid-air, and points it toward the screen like a remote control. Clicking furiously, he turns to you and says, "See! Nothing is happening! And that arrow thingy isn't even moving!" How do you respond to this gentleman? In this chapter, we suggest how best to protect this person's feelings *and* the sale.

Meet the Customer Where He Is

You are clearly seeing an example of someone who lacks the ability to use a computer. He does not see it this way, though. In his mind, he just made an expensive purchase that should have better directions and be easier to use, just like his television set or his telephone. And, in a sense, he is right! So start the conversation by validating his view of the world, as outlined in Chapter 3:

"You're right. Computers can be incredibly frustrating to use. Let's look into this."

Notice that we are not starting the conversation by saying that people have trouble using computers. This would be placing the fault on the customer before we even investigate the problem. After you test the computer and make sure everything is working properly, you then can begin to discuss the issue of learning to use a computer by normalizing it, as discussed in Chapter 7:

"Computers often require instruction to use for the first time, especially if you're new to them. I have some great options that I could discuss with you. First, I'd like to learn a little more about how you would like to use this system."

A particularly powerful form of normalizing is the "I" technique that we described in Chapter 4, where we frame things in terms of our own experience:

"I found computers like these to be really confusing when I first started using them too. Here are some things that helped me come up to speed with them. . . ."

Explore the Deeper Question

Note that the statements above included a question about how this person wanted to use his computer. He may want to communicate online with his grandchildren, check his investments in the stock market, or write his next book in a world that no longer accepts typewritten manuscripts. Whatever he tells you is valuable data that will help inform your responses to him.

Once you know this customer's reasons for using a computer, you can explore appropriate solutions. If he needs to become comfortable with a word processor and email, for example, computer training may be in order. If he simply wants to play games or chat online, a simpler device, like a tablet computer, may be more appropriate. For some tasks, you could even explore whether a knowledgeable member of his household could work with him once you help him set up the computer. Learn what his real wishes are, and then partner with him to help make them happen.

Make the Customer Feel Good

Finally, the most subtle point here is that this customer was really annoying at first. His behavior was a perfect trifecta when he came into your store: arrogant, wrong, and not terribly well-informed. Human nature often leads us to "correct" customers like this one—and when we do, we often pay a price in bad reactions and lost business. Instead, start thinking how to make this customer feel good for giving you his business.

In the middle of his bluster, this customer has handed you several important pieces of information. He used to be a professor. He feels he is intelligent (and perhaps, by corollary, doesn't feel appreciated for it at his age). He is persistent enough to keep returning computers. You can leverage these facts to help build a relationship, by doing things like:

- Asking about what he used to teach as a professor
- Normalizing the situation by mentioning other intelligent people you know who had issues when first using a computer
- Talking about how much he will enjoy doing what he plans to do with the system
- Sharing how someone with his talents often learns quickly
- Giving him credit for trying hard to resolve the issue

In Chapter 10, we talked about reaffirming the customer relationship, or even thanking a difficult customer, as you wrap up the transaction. By helping this customer feel good about a potentially embarrassing situation, and by helping this product benefit him, you may well gain an appreciative customer for life.

PART IV

Beyond the Worst Case

CHAPTER 19

When Talking Isn't Enough: Keeping Yourself and Your Customer Safe

DID YOU KNOW that increasing the price of your fast food can be dangerous? According to a March 2011 article in the *Colorado Springs (CO) Gazette*, after a man picked up seven crunchy beef burritos at a restaurant and discovered that each of them now cost fifty cents more, he fired at an employee with an air rifle. After police were called, he fired at officers with an assault rifle and barricaded himself in a hotel room before being charged with attempted murder.

On the one hand, serving the public is statistically one of the safest professions you can choose. According to the Bureau of Labor Statistics and the National Lightning Safety Institute, you are almost twenty times more likely to be struck by lightning than to die at the hands of a customer. On the other hand, an average of about sixty people are killed by customers every year in the United States, and hundreds more are injured. Customer rage can be aimed at anyone, no matter how well he or she communicates, for reasons that range from extreme frustration to mental instability.

As a result, every person (and every employer) who serves the public needs a safety plan for recognizing serious issues, calling for help, and physically removing oneself from a dangerous situation. In this chapter, we explore how you can tell when a customer situation is getting out of hand and what to do to keep yourself safe.

Situational Awareness: Trusting Your Gut

This book focuses on the idea that saying the right things, at the right time, can calm down a difficult situation. At the same time, it is a dangerous fallacy to believe that you can talk your way out of anything. Sadly, there are people who have bad intentions or cannot be reasoned with, and situations where communications skills alone are not sufficient. As a result, an important part of your tool kit for serving the public is developing a skill we refer to as *situational awareness*, a term originally applied to military conflict scenarios. It involves becoming aware of your surroundings and trusting your own perceptions when a situation might get out of hand. Here are some examples of putting it into action:

▶ Someone who comes into your retail store acts unusually agitated or evasive. You respond by making eye contact with the customer and acknowledging him, and by getting a colleague on the floor as backup.

▶ A group of rough-looking teenagers at your video arcade are loud and disruptive. You alert security in case their behavior shifts to damaging property or harassing other customers.

▶ One of the patients at your psychiatric hospital has just received the news that her regular counselor has left for a new position. The patient is very upset about this and is not eating or sleeping well. You make sure that you and others on your team treat this patient with caring and compassion during what is likely to be a difficult transition period.

In each of these cases, you actively look for cues that might concern you, or situations that fall far outside your norms. Some of these might include:

- ▶ Visible agitation or distress

- ▶ Avoiding eye contact or trying to stay invisible

- ▶ A disregard for the rules or norms of your establishment

- ▶ Talking incoherently or suspiciously

- ▶ A stated or unstated sense of powerlessness on the part of the customer

- ▶ Situations with major consequences for the customer

- ▶ A group of people who appear to be threatening or confrontational

This is where the second and perhaps most important part of situational awareness comes in: trusting your gut when it tells you to be careful, or to take action. It may feel funny to call for help when a boisterous group of people may just be celebrating a football victory, or to get backup when a visibly upset customer may have simply had an argument with a spouse. But when things go wrong, it often happens because we underreact instead of overreact to a situation. So listen closely to that voice inside your head, and take what it tells you seriously.

The Disorderly Customer

Not all difficult customers are necessarily angry ones. People may act out or cause a disturbance for a wide range of reasons, including mental health issues, having too much to drink, or being part of a "wolf pack" intent on causing trouble. How do you try to keep these situations under control?

Lieutenant Chauncey Bennett III of the New York State University Police, who has plenty of experience dealing with disorderly people on college campuses, recommends a calm and nonthreatening approach: "Use good nonverbal body language, such as keeping your open palms visible, as you approach people and start talking with them. If they respond in a way that is irrational or threatening, use statements like,

'Please know I am here to help you . . . can you allow me to do that?' or 'Is there anything I can say or do to avoid this situation getting worse so that I can help you?'"

When verbal techniques are not effective, Bennett trains people to recognize "fight or flight" body movements in other people, such as transitioning to terse or monosyllabic answers, making less eye contact, looking around quickly or looking "through" you, or clenching their fists or jaw muscles. These are danger signals that the situation may escalate into a physical confrontation. In cases like these, he recommends increasing the distance between you and the other person, continuing to keep your palms open and visible, and giving the person the choice between allowing you to help versus calling for assistance.

So what happens when an entire group is acting disorderly? Bennett feels that situations like that should be left to professionals with appropriate tools at their disposal. Here is how these professionals often intervene: "We frequently try to identify the group leader, take that person to the side, and explain that we need their help to assure a positive outcome to this situation. By building rapport, and letting them know that we will work to assist them if they help us calm down the situation, we can often very quickly bring some order to a disorderly incident."

Reacting to Risk

What are your choices when a customer's behavior doesn't feel right to you, or starts to cross the line from difficult to unsafe?

When things go wrong on an airplane, such as the loss of an engine, pilots have a checklist they follow to manage the emergency. Ideally, you want to have a checklist for your most threatening situations as well, one that helps mitigate the possible risk for you and your customer. Here are some possible courses of action.

Make Your Presence Known

When customers act suspiciously—and particularly in cases where you feel they may be planning theft or vandalism—retailers often advise greeting these customers or at least making eye contact with them to let them know you are aware of them.

Bring in Backup

There is safety in numbers. When you have more than one person visible and on duty, it proactively lessens the possibility that a customer will act out dangerously and provides more staff to handle a situation.

Maintain Physical Space

Normally, being physically close to a customer shows interest. When someone is acting suspiciously, however, keeping a safe distance increases your reaction time and provides a margin of safety in case a customer starts to react.

Know Your Escape Routes

A good rule of thumb is to never let an upset customer get between you and your path of exit. For example, psychotherapists who work with potentially dangerous patients generally make it a point to sit between the patient and the door, and often have access to a panic button that alerts others to a critical situation.

Speak to the Other Person's Interest

When hostage negotiators show up at the scene of a crisis situation, the first thing they usually do is check in with the hostage taker and offer to help. Do not presume that words alone are sufficient to manage a true crisis, but when you must speak, maintain a calm and helpful presence, even as you attempt to set boundaries.

Good crisis managers know how to normalize situations, by framing them with words that make things seem normal and beneficial to the customer. For instance, a neighbor of mine who works in retail security often tells shoplifters he catches that it would be more beneficial to come back to the store with him rather than having him call the police—and usually they come willingly. By taking situations where most of us get tense and bark out orders, and instead turning them into productive dialogue, we help everyone calm down and de-escalate the situation.

Words That Saved a Life

If someone was on a murderous rampage, would you be able to talk him into keeping you both safe? Even though what follows is not a customer situation, it has important lessons for how service professionals should react in a crisis.

When waitress Ashley Smith came home late one night from her shift at an Atlanta-area restaurant in March 2005, she had no idea that the man accosting her in the parking lot had killed five people over the course of a day that started with a dramatic courthouse rampage and escape. While tied up and held hostage in her apartment, she tried to calm the man down by sharing stories of her own tough life. Soon he trusted her enough to untie her. As he watched the drama of the police hunt for him unfold on television, she encouraged him by saying that his situation was not hopeless and sharing stories from the Bible and the book *The Purpose-Driven Life*. Later she offered to cook him breakfast and further earned his trust by helping him dispose of his stolen truck.

Within several hours, the suspect finally allowed her to leave her apartment, after which she contacted the authorities and he was apprehended without incident. According to a police spokesperson, she survived because she "managed to make a rapport with him and made herself a person, not just an object."

Don't Go It Alone: Have a Safety Plan

When it comes to keeping yourself safe with customers, perhaps the most important advice is to get everyone in your organization on the same page. An organization is only as strong as its weakest link, and crisis-management skills are useless if only a chosen few people know them.

If you work with the public, you and your organization should have a safety plan that teaches everyone what to do in an emergency. For a customer-contact organization, elements of a good safety plan might include the following:

- ▶ **Crisis prevention.** Teach people how to recognize situations that have the potential to erupt, together with guidelines to try to prevent them from happening in the first place.

- ▶ **How to react in common crisis situations.** For example, many retail organizations have a policy of not fighting or resisting robbers, knowing that a single misguided employee could provoke reactions that get people hurt or killed.

- ▶ **Your communications plan.** Make sure everyone knows whom to call, with up-to-date contact information, including the order of preference in which people should be contacted. Be sure to include outside authorities such as police, fire, or paramedics.

- ▶ **What to say and not say.** Human nature often takes over in a crisis, but when it leads people to respond with anger or agitation, the result can be a very bad outcome. Teach people how to respond in ways that defuse the situation.

- ▶ **Physical safety.** Document ways to evacuate or retreat to a secure location in the event that a situation becomes dangerous.

Remember, working with the public is generally very safe. Many, if not most, customer-contact professionals will go through their entire careers and never encounter a truly dangerous situation. And good communications skills, like the ones you are learning in this book, can go a long way toward keeping things safe in the first place. But with a small amount of planning and preparation, you and your team can be better equipped to help even crisis situations come to a successful resolution.

CHAPTER 20

From Customer Crisis to Excellent Service: Lessons for the Whole Organization

MANY PEOPLE look at the skills in this book as mainly being important for one thing: handling difficult customer situations. I would like you to rethink this idea.

My experience is that the benefits of critical customer skills go far beyond customer interactions. Deployed properly, as part of an integrated approach to training, coaching, and employee orientation, these tools can fundamentally change the morale, turnover, service quality, and success of your entire workplace. As we close, let's look at how you can use crisis communications skills as a foundation for success.

Creating a Service Culture

Every workplace on the face of the earth will tell you that it should deliver good customer service. In my view—and more important, my experience—teaching everyone critical customer skills is the key to making this happen.

Many organizations mistakenly believe that good service is a matter of attitude. Yet it is difficult, if not impossible, to succeed by asking grown men and women to change their attitudes. In my experience as a manager and consultant, real change comes from creating a culture of continuous growth and learning—in other words, by teaching people valuable life skills and making them part of something bigger than themselves.

People fundamentally do not like being told how to feel or how to behave. At the same time, most of us love learning new skills that improve our lives. And when you give everyone the same kinds of skills that other crisis professionals use, you give them the gift of confidence and leadership. This, in turn, always leads to dramatically better service.

Watch Me Handle This

Once I was shadowing agents at a large call-center operation as part of a consulting visit. As soon as I sat down with one woman a customer came on the line, and it was clear that he wasn't happy—because I could hear him shouting right through the earpiece of her headset. Then this agent put him on hold, turned to me with a smile, and said quietly, "Watch me handle this."

Then she went back to the call and nailed it with the perfection of Michael Jordan sinking a three-pointer. She acknowledged his frustrations, validated his concerns, and laid out his options in a way that made her sound like his best friend and advocate.

In my own career of managing customer support operations, sometimes when an upset customer would demand to "speak to the manager"—that would be me—some of my agents would sit in my office and listen to us talk on the speakerphone. Of course, my goal was to send the customer away happy. But I also had another equally important objective: showing my team how to go into these situations with confidence.

Managing Internal Conflict

Do you work with people who gossip? Are backstabbers? Create drama on a regular basis? Or perhaps have retired on the job and forgot to tell you about it?

Guess what? All of these people are difficult customers too—difficult internal customers. And the way you address these energy-sapping, productivity-killing behaviors is by using exactly the same kinds of communications skills that you use with difficult external customers.

Scratch the surface of most workplaces and you will usually find these behaviors being handled through anger, frustration, or punishment. Unfortunately, these approaches rarely work well. But when people learn to speak to the interests and positions of others, using strength-based communication, everything changes.

When I am called in as a therapist to do workplace interventions with teams in conflict, the vast majority of my work involves using exactly the same kinds of communications skills taught in this book for handling challenging customer situations. By learning and practicing these skills, employees and managers alike can become their own "therapists" and help create a more harmonious and productive workplace.

How to Talk to a Backstabber

In live workshops, I often ask attendees how they would talk to people who are "stabbing them in the back"—in other words, saying negative things about them to others. Their answers are almost always the same: Confront them, call them on their behavior, and demand they stop it.

Next, I ask for a show of hands of how many of them have never, ever expressed an opinion about someone at work. No one ever raises a hand, of course. Then I point out that although I intentionally used the emotionally charged phrase "stabbing them in the back" to describe this behavior, in reality it is something nearly everyone normally does.

> Then we look at what they might say in order to productively open dialogue, and often end up with something like this: "You probably don't feel you get a fair shake here. You might think some people get breaks that you don't. You probably even talk about people here to others, just like I do. I'd like to see if there are ways we could work together in the future so I could support you. What do you think?"

Personal Growth

I speak forty to fifty times a year all over North America. Do you know what the most common comment is that I hear from these audiences after I speak?

"I can't wait to try these techniques at home!"

There is actually some good science behind this statement. Many of the techniques described in this book spring from theories of marriage and family therapy, designed around working with couples and families in conflict. The same skills that calm down customers can also open dialogue with your partner, your parents, your teenagers, or your mother-in-law.

So if you teach your team members how to defuse customer conflict, you are giving them skills that impact the rest of their lives in a positive way. Their daily work with customers reinforces these skills and helps them foster good family and workplace relationships, which in turn leads to happier employees. It is a win-win situation that costs the organization little or nothing.

This point was driven home to me recently after I had taught a workshop in acknowledgment skills. One workshop participant came up to me with a broad smile of recognition on her face. She exclaimed, "Now I finally understand my husband! He is an interrogator with a national law enforcement agency, and he is so good with people. No one can ever get in an argument with him!" (Hopefully, she can now match him skill for skill at the dinner table.) Crisis skills are life enhancing, and with the right environment at work, they can become contagious.

Communicating as an Organization

Finally, communications skills for difficult situations can often become the hallmark of a great organization, particularly in its most critical and public moments.

History is full of examples of corporations that issued short-sighted and self-serving statements that damaged their public reputations, often at the worst possible times. By contrast, good crisis communication has often been part of the signature moments of many companies. Witness, for example, the very public and detailed apology from JetBlue's CEO after hundreds of its passengers were stranded in an ice storm in 2007, or how Johnson & Johnson handled the Tylenol-tampering scandal of the 1980s. The very same skills we discuss in this book for customer crises, such as owning criticism and acknowledging other people's positions, apply at the highest level of the boardroom as well.

At a deeper level, organizations also brand themselves in the ways that they communicate day in and day out with their employees. Understanding how to use language effectively can serve as an antidote to the bland, infuriating corporate twaddle that often announces changes ranging from new rules to layoffs. The same skills that create good customer service, when deployed across an entire organization, can form the foundation for a workplace that is liked and trusted by everyone.

Creating an Organizational Apology

In 1987, it came to light that Chrysler Motors had sold as new cars vehicles that had actually been test-driven by its managers with the odometers disconnected, and even in some cases damaged in accidents and repaired. This led to substantial negative publicity and declining showroom traffic.

In the face of this crisis, Chrysler's then-chairman, Lee Iacocca, crafted a legendary apology. He expressed concern for Chrysler's customers and their faith in the company, promised to make things right, and then took complete ownership for what happened in refreshingly blunt language: "We did do something to make our customers question their faith in us—two things, in fact. . . . The first thing was just dumb, [and] the second, I think, went beyond dumb, and reached all the way out to stupid." He then closed by apologizing and promising that the situation would never happen again.

According to communications expert John Kador, author of the book *Effective Apology*, Iacocca's handling of this customer-satisfaction crisis was pitch-perfect. "First, he acknowledged that the customer had a legitimate grievance. Second, he accepted full responsibility, effectively saying that, 'I agree with you. We messed up.' Third, he apologized by being very direct, without equivocation."

The net result was that Chrysler ultimately survived the crisis. As Kador notes, "If you empathize, admit the error, accept responsibility, say you're sorry, provide restitution, and promise not to do it again, you will find that most customers will be incredibly forgiving and become stronger allies for your brand."

The Bottom Line

If I could choose just one thing that would create happy customers, happy employees, sales increases, and successful organizations, it would be teaching everyone how to communicate successfully with their most difficult customers. The reason I am so passionate about these skills is that I have seen them work so well, and so consistently, for organizations I have managed and consulted for.

There is a personal side to this journey for me. I grew up extremely conflict avoidant. The thought of being confronted by people was incredibly frightening for me. Early in life, I felt that the ability to handle difficult situations was the exclusive domain of people who were somehow stronger, braver, or smarter than I was. As I grew into adulthood and studied psychology, it was a life-changing gift to discover that these talents were simply a matter of linguistics. And today I live a very happy life putting myself into the worst customer service situations you can imagine, week after week.

My goal is to give the same gift to you and to your organization—the gift of confidence. And the gift of effective negotiation. And the gift of organizational growth. And, above all, the gift of sending more customers away happy than you could have ever imagined possible. Use it, teach it, and spread it far and wide. Best of success!

Solutions to Putting Learning into Practice Exercises

Chapter 2: Leaning Into Criticism

1. You work for a large rental company. A customer marches in and says, "The tent you put up for us leaked and everyone got drenched, along with their meals! You've completely ruined our son's graduation party." What is your response?

A: Paraphrase the situation: "My goodness, it sounds like this made a complete mess of your big event! Tell me more about what happened."

2. The utility company you work for mistakenly sent disconnection notices to several thousand people because of a computer error, and—lucky you—you are on the phones today answering one call after another from customers who are furious about this. What is the first thing you say to each person?

A: Mirror the person's emotions: "We made a mistake that has been incredibly frustrating for you and thousands of other customers, and we want to apologize for that."

3. You are a young doctor and get a surprise visit from a patient you saw yesterday. "Look at me!" she exclaims. She is covered from head to toe in a rash caused by the medication you prescribed for her the day before. What do you say now?

A: Steal her best lines: "Wow, this medication has had some terrible side effects for you! How are you feeling right now?"

Chapter 3: Achieving Deep Acknowledgment

1. A customer storms up to you and declares, "Your crew did a terrible job of landscaping on my property! See how uneven this line of shrubs is? I'm going to tell all my neighbors to stay away from your company!" How might you paraphrase what she is saying?

A: "It sounds like we didn't do what you were expecting at all here, starting with these shrubs. Tell me more."

2. How would you make an observation about what she is thinking and feeling?

A: "We obviously made you very unhappy with this job."

3. What might you say to validate her feelings?

A: "No one wants his or her home to look bad."

4. What could you say that would show her that you personally identify with her, in a way that doesn't bash your employer?

A: "I wouldn't want my own property to look less than perfect either. Let's see what we can do here."

Chapter 4: Avoiding Trigger Phrases

1. A customer's child is running amok in your store, pulling merchandise off the shelves and throwing it around. What do you say to the parent?

A: Don't give orders to the customer: "Your child is obviously having a good time. Let's try to distract him from the merchandise together."

2. A customer finally gets to the front of a line, but it turns out to be the wrong one. Now you have to tell him that he must wait in yet another long line. What can you say that won't make this person angry?

A: Avoid blaming the customer or using catchphrases like "I'm sorry": "I know exactly where you need to go for this. Unfortunately, it involves one more line, and I apologize that you had to wait in this one. The clerk handling that line over there will be able to take care of you."

3.   A customer is angrily complaining that his new digital camera doesn't work. As he demonstrates the problem, it is clear that he is pressing the wrong button to try to turn it on. What do you first say to him?

A: Normalize the situation: "These cameras confuse lots of people. I see this all the time. Let me show you how to get this working."

4.   A woman is talking loudly on her cell phone in the dining room of the golf club where you work. This is against the rules of the club, and other people are complaining. How can you "educate" this person without being insulting?

A: Avoid using a one-sided explanation: "Since our dining room is a quiet zone, we have an area outside the dining room where you can use your cell phone freely. I'll be glad to show you where you can go when you need to take a call."

Chapter 5: Divide and Conquer: The Safe Way to Deliver Bad News

1.   Someone is trying to return a broken laptop to your store for a refund. The screen is cracked, there is a muddy footprint on it, and it is clear that the customer caused the damage. What might be a good way to begin your response?

A: Use a good introduction to frame the situation: "It looks like you had some accidental damage here. Let me walk you through what the warranty covers in a situation like this."

2.   What kind of explanation might you give about refusing him a refund?

A: Give lots of details: "We do have warranties that cover accidental damage. They cost extra and have to be purchased before an incident like this. In your case, you have a manufacturer's warranty that covers defects in the product—for example, if it came from the factory not working. Because damaged merchandise is nonreturnable, we'll need to look at some options beyond the warranty coverage here."

3.   The customer responds by complaining about how expensive laptops are and wondering why a big, profitable chain like yours can't just take this computer back. How would you reply?

A: Give an empathetic response. "You're right, laptops are a big expense. I wish we had better coverage for accidents like this. No one expects situations like this to happen after spending this much money. I don't blame you for trying to return this."

4. What options might you offer this customer to try to make the best of the situation?

A: **Review the options as an ally.** "Here are some options that might lessen the financial impact of this situation. First, even though the screen is damaged, the rest of the computer appears to be working. If you wish, an inexpensive converter might allow you to still use this computer with another monitor or your television set. Second, even broken computers do have some salvage value, and people sometimes sell them via channels such as eBay. Third, you might explore taking a tax deduction for this situation as a casualty loss or a business expense. Depending on your tax bracket, this might represent a substantial discount on your next computer. Finally, given what happened, I would be willing to offer you our best discount if you decide to purchase a new computer."

Chapter 6: Powerful Problem Solving: Beyond "Yes We Can" and "No We Can't"

1. Your valet parking attendant just dented a customer's expensive car. The owner is demanding a brand new car, claiming that you "ruined" it and that it will never be right again. How do you respond?

A: **After apologizing for the damage, acknowledge the customer's view as he sees it and focus on what you can do:** "This is a really expensive, high-performance car, and I would certainly want this situation to be made whole if it were me too. The least we can do is have this damage assessed by an expert who can get your input. What dealer do you normally work with?"

2. A customer is complaining that he and his family were forced to sit in front of several loud, drunken fans at your ballpark, and is demanding a refund of everyone's tickets. You have a no-refund policy. What would you say in response to his demands for a refund?

A: **Acknowledge the customer and paint a better future:** "It sounds like you and your family had a miserable time. Here are a couple of things we can do for you. First, if you ever come back to the ballpark again, I want you to know that our security team is here to help you if you ever run into a situation like this again—just stop by this office. Second, even though we have a no-refund policy, I would like to offer you a discount voucher, because it would be great to have you come back and enjoy another game with us."

3.   Someone insists on cutting ahead of a long line because she is in a rush. What could you say to her?

A: Use the transitional phrase "even though" to focus on solutions: "It looks like you're in a rush. Even though we have to help these people first, we can probably get to you within the next ten minutes. Would that work for you?" (If the answer is "no," explore other options: stating how late you are open, calling in an order, and so on.)

4.   A young man was ordered to leave your store after shouting and cursing at your employees when he was refused a refund. Now his mother, who has only heard his side of the story, has come in demanding a formal apology. How might you first address her?

A: Validate the mother's agenda and ask to hear her view of the situation: "No one wants to feel like their child was disrespected. How did he describe the situation to you?" If you later correct her version of events, do so empathetically: "Your son was probably very upset, and may not have even realized how he was reacting. We certainly want to be fair both to him and to our employees. If he can express his concerns in the future without resorting to shouting and foul language, we would be happy to welcome him back to our store again."

Chapter 7: Reframing Your Message

1.   You are going to arrive much later than expected for a plumbing appointment. You know from experience that this customer gets upset about everything. What could you say to lessen the intensity of his reaction?

A: Use normalizing: "Sometimes we have unexpected delays with plumbing problems, so today we're running a lot later than I would like. The good news is that I can still get to you today, if you wish. Would it work for you if I came around 4 p.m.?"

2.   A season ticket holder of the professional football team you work for is being informed that his seats are being moved to a less-desirable section so more luxury boxes can be built at your stadium. How would you deliver this news?

A: Use relative value: "Despite the impact of the construction, we will be able to relocate you to a section that is within the same quadrant of the stadium, within four rows of your original seats."

3.   You are telling one of the patients at your clinic that she has been reported to a credit bureau for not paying her bill on time. How would you word this?

A: Use context framing: "This is a very common situation, and as long as we can work with you to get current on your balance, there shouldn't be a long-term impact on your credit."

4.   A customer is extremely loud and abrasive as she describes a haircut she felt went badly at your salon. Your manager hears this and rushes over. How would you explain the situation to the manager?

A: Use neutral terms to describe the customer's behavior, but do not minimize her concerns: "Sally was sharing her concerns with me about a haircut that she was extremely unhappy about."

Chapter 8: Grounding an Angry Outburst

For all three of these scenarios, the approach is similar: (a) use the highest level of acknowledgment possible, (b) ask good assessment questions, and (c) shift the focus to problem solving.

1.   You are a hospital administrator, and a mother is furious about her son's treatment: the delays, the pain, the lack of communication. How should you respond?

A: "Being in a hospital is frightening enough. I certainly wouldn't want my child to be in pain, and in the dark, in a situation like this, so I'm very glad you came to see me. First, let me ask: How is your son doing right now? Is he still in pain? Next, I would like to learn more about what happened here. I really appreciate your input. Now, what can we do to make things right for your son for the rest of his stay?"

2.   One of your home-remodeling clients calls, enraged that your crew accidentally shattered a prized stained glass window at her house. This situation was totally your fault. How do you respond?

A: "I can't even imagine how upset you must be about having such a beautiful window damaged. I remember it well, and it is one of the showpieces of your house. First, I want to sincerely apologize for such a terrible mishap. Now, could you describe the damage for me? How much of the window was affected? Are there any safety issues I should know about, like sharp edges of glass? . . . I want to stop by as soon as possible to see what we can do to make this right. When would be a good time for you?"

3. A woman is very angry about her lawn mower breaking down again. After you have asked a few questions, it is clear to you that she is misusing it on terrain it was never intended for. Nonetheless, she feels the problem is your fault. What do you say?

A: "I can see how frustrated you are—this is probably the fourth time you've had to bring this mower back for repairs! So let's try to get to the bottom of this. Tell me about the area you are mowing. Is it flat? Are there any roots or branches under your path? What are the grass and the vegetation like? . . . I think I see where the problem might be. You are describing the kind of terrain that we normally use a heavy-duty mower for. Let me walk you through some options."

Chapter 9: Becoming Immune to Intimidation

1. You run a small wholesale business, and a new customer is offering you a large contract, but he tells you your prices are ridiculous and insists on a 40 percent discount, similar to what he says everyone else would offer him. You still would like his business. What do you say in response?

A: Accept his self-importance: "It sounds like you do a good job of watching your costs. Let me go over what kinds of quantity discounts I can offer you on premium stock items like these."

2. You explain to a customer that she will need to pay for a repair, and she replies tartly, "I don't usually deal with people at your level anyway." What is your reply?

A: Use fogging: "Sometimes people do want to speak to a manager about situations like these, and you are welcome to do so. I apologize that I can't waive the repair fee."

3. A diner expresses dissatisfaction with his meal and wants you to cancel the bill for his entire party of eight. He is threatening to contact a local food critic if you don't. How do you respond to this?

A: Underreact to the threat: "I apologize that you weren't happy with your meal, and I wouldn't dream of telling you whom not to talk to. If it would help, I am prepared to offer you a discount on tonight's bill."

Chapter 10: The Wrap-Up

1. A customer angrily demanded a refund for a product after going on at great length about how horrible it was. She didn't realize that you would be more

than happy to give her a refund, and now she looks a little embarrassed about her behavior. What do you say?

A: Normalize the situation: "Situations like these frustrate a lot of people. In fact, I reacted very similarly when I was having constant problems with my food processor. I'm glad we could work this out."

2. Someone calls your appliance service company and is extremely upset that no one showed up as scheduled the day before to make a repair. After rescheduling the appointment, what do you say before hanging up?

A: Provide a verbal receipt: "Let's reconfirm what our plans are for tomorrow. We are going to make sure that someone arrives between noon and 2 p.m. at your house. In the event there are any delays, one of our staff will call you at your home number. And I want to encourage you to check in with me personally if there are any problems tomorrow. Finally, I want to apologize again for what happened yesterday, and we really appreciate your giving us a chance to make this situation right."

3. A woman purchased several expensive pieces of equipment at your hardware store and was very picky and demanding about everything. You sense that she was getting exasperated with you as she kept pressing you with more questions. What might you say at the end of the transaction to help preserve her future business?

A: Reaffirm the customer relationship: "You've picked out some very good-quality pieces of equipment, and I'm glad we could help you. Please come back if we can help you with anything else in the future."

References

Chapter 1: Understanding the "Uh-Oh" Moment

Shakespeare, William. *Julius Caesar*, act 3, sc. 2.

Chapter 5: Divide and Conquer: The Safe Way to Deliver Bad News

Davis, Dr. Nancy. "Death Notification Training Video." Accessed July 4, 2012. http://drnancydavis.com/home/death-notification-training-video.

Chapter 8: Grounding an Angry Outburst

Frank, Robert. "Chinese Millionaire Smashes His Lamborghini." *Wall Street Journal* blogs, March 18, 2011. http://blogs.wsj.com/wealth/2011/03/18/chinese-millionaire-smashes-his-200000-lamborghini/.

Berger, Joseph. "Years Later, Lawsuit Seeks to Recreate a Wedding." *New York Times*, November 2, 2011.

Shaw, Russell. "75-Year-Old Woman Smashes Up Local Comcast Office with Hammer." *ZDNet.com*, October 18, 2007. http://www.zdnet.com/blog/ip-telephony/75-year-old-woman-smashes-up-local-comcast-office-with-hammer/2605.

Chapter 9: Becoming Immune to Intimidation

Roth, Carol. *The Entrepreneur Equation: Evaluating the Realities, Risks, and Rewards of Having Your Own Business*. Dallas: BenBella, 2011.

Smith, Manuel J. *When I Say No, I Feel Guilty*. New York: Bantam, 1975.

Chapter 14: I'll Be Suing You

Phillips Law Firm. "Medical Malpractice: Study Shows That Doctors Admitting Fault Lowers Number of Lawsuits," August 2010. http://

www.justiceforyou.com/2010/08/medical-malpractice-study-shows-that-doctors-admitting-fault-lowers-number-of-lawsuits/.

Kachalia, Allen, MD; Samuel L. Kaufman MA; Richard Boothman JD; Susan Anderson MBA, MSN; Kathleen Welch MBA, MPH; Sanjay Saint MD, MPH; and Mary A.M. Rogers PhD. "Liability Claims and Costs Before and After Implementation of a Medical Error Disclosure Program." *Annals of Internal Medicine*, August 17, 2010, 153(4):213–221.

Chapter 15: Quelling a Social Media Firestorm

Carroll, Dave. "United Breaks Guitars" video. YouTube. Accessed July 7, 2012. http://www.youtube.com/watch?v=5YGc4zOqozo, posted July 6, 2009.

Chapter 19: When Talking Isn't Enough: Keeping Yourself and Your Customer Safe

Colorado Springs (CO) Gazette. "Taco Bell Customer Shoots at Employees, Police over Burrito Price Increase," March 22, 2011. http://www.gazette.com/articles/bell-114916-price-burrito.html.

Bureau of Labor Statistics. "Occupational Homicides by Selected Characteristics, 1997–2010." Accessed July 4, 2012. http://www.bls.gov/iif/oshwc/cfoi/work_hom.pdf.

National Lightning Safety Institute. "Lightning Strike Probabilities." Accessed July 4, 2012. http://www.lightningsafety.com/nlsi_pls/probability.html.

CBS News. "Atlanta Hostage Recounts Ordeal," March 14, 2005. http://www.cbsnews.com/stories/2005/03/14/national/main679837.shtml.

Chapter 20: From Customer Crisis to Excellent Service: Lessons for the Whole Organization

Chicago Tribune. "JetBlue Issues Apology in Ads," February 22, 2007. http://articles.chicagotribune.com/2007-02-22/news/0702220380_1_david-neeleman-jetblue-airways-bryan-baldwin.

Drolet, Danielle. "80s Tylenol Scare Still a Model Crisis Case Study." *PRWeek*, May 20, 2011. http://www.prweekus.com/80s-tylenol-scare-still-a-model-crisis-case-study/article/203351/.

Kador, John. *Effective Apology: Mending Fences, Building Bridges, and Restoring Trust.* San Francisco: Berrett-Koehler, 2009.

Risen, James. "Iacocca Admits Mileage Tampering Was 'Dumb': Apologizes for Chrysler's New Car 'Test-Drives' by Its Managers with Odometers Disconnected," *Los Angeles Times*, July 2, 1987. http://articles.latimes.com/1987-07-02/business/fi-1822_1_test-cars.

Index

About the Author

RICH GALLAGHER MA, MFT is one of the nation's leading experts on workplace communications skills. His nine books include *What to Say to a Porcupine: 20 Humorous Tales That Get to the Heart of Great Customer Service* (AMACOM, 2008), a national number one customer service and business humor bestseller and finalist for 800-CEO-READ's 2008 Business Book Awards in the Fables category; as well as *How to Tell Anyone Anything: Breakthrough Techniques for Handling Difficult Conversations at Work* (AMACOM, 2009).

A former customer service executive and practicing psychotherapist as well as a popular public speaker, Gallagher focuses on the mechanics of what to say in difficult situations, based on the latest principles of behavioral psychology. His track record includes helping to lead a West Coast software startup to become a major NASDAQ company as its director of customer services, as well as leading a 24/7 call center to near-perfect customer satisfaction and near-zero turnover. His training and development firm, Point of Contact Group, has taught over twenty thousand people how to take control of any interpersonal situation.

Gallagher is a member of the National Speakers Association, and he is a veteran of numerous speaking engagements, media appearances, and corporate workshops. He also was the subject-matter expert for the American Management Association's Communication Boot Camp program. Visit him at www.pointofcontactgroup.com.